28

Some Male Offenders' Problems

I.   Homeless Offenders in Liverpool
     By W. McWilliams

II. Casework with Short-term Prisoners
     By Julie Holborn

LONDON: HER MAJESTY'S STATIONERY OFFICE

ISBN 0 11 340668 1

FOREWORD

This volume contains two reports about problems encountered by some male offenders. Both authors have now left the Research Unit.

Homeless offenders in Liverpool is the outcome of research planned after discussions with the Liverpool Probation and After-Care Service and the North-West Regional Group Consultative Committee for after-care hostels. Mr. McWilliams began the study while a probation officer in Liverpool, and the Liverpool Probation and After-Care Committee seconded him to the Home Office Research Unit to complete it and to assist with the more extensive programme of research of which the study forms part. The study describes an attempt to identify characteristics of samples of homeless male offenders; to illustrate some of the problems they present; and to examine the attitudes of probation officers involved in their treatment. The study was limited in that the sampling was restricted to the area of the Liverpool Probation and After-Care Service: consequently the detailed findings may not apply elsewhere, but they were used in setting up an experimental study of prisoners under the title 'IMPACT—Liverpool'.

Casework with short-term prisoners reports an exploratory study whose object was to refine criteria for selecting men for the welfare service offered in prison and to develop methods of working with them. There was no control group in this study; the report is based on interviews about their experiences of prison welfare and after-care, with 120 men serving short sentences in three Midland prisons.

I. J. CROFT
Head of the Research Unit

January 1975

CONTENTS

TABLES

I: HOMELESS OFFENDERS IN LIVERPOOL

NOTE:

Where information is not available for all members of a sample that is the
subject of a Table, the cases affected have been excluded from that Table.

CONTENTS

TABLES

II: CASEWORK WITH SHORT-TERM PRISONERS

ix

I. HOMELESS OFFENDERS IN LIVERPOOL

by
W. McWilliams

ACKNOWLEDGEMENTS

To Mr. R. V. Johnson and the staff at the Liverpool After-Care Unit I owe a particular debt of gratitude for completing the schedules and always being ready to enter into discussions about their own cases and homeless offenders in general.

The interest shown in the research by Mr. R. E. Gaze, the Principal Probation Officer, and by members of his staff was warmly appreciated, as was the time given by so many officers in helping me to understand more clearly the problems of homeless men.

For the first year of the study I was employed directly by the Liverpool Probation and After-Care Service, and during the early stages of the work the project was assisted by discussions with Dr. Martin Davies, then a member of the Home Office Research Unit. I am also grateful to a number of colleagues for their comments and advice at various stages in the work.

WILLIAM McWILLIAMS

SECTION I

Introduction

A good deal of attention has been given in recent years to the problems presented to the penal system by homeless offenders. The work of a number of voluntary bodies such as the National Association for the Care and Resettlement of Offenders, the publication of the Reading Report[1], and the subsequent setting up by the Home Office of Regional Group Consultative Committees to study the accommodation needs of offenders in different regions are all indications of the concern which has been felt for the situation of men and women offenders who are without homes. The problems encountered in providing appropriately for their needs on an individual basis have been described by Turner[2] and other writers, and few people would now underestimate the difficulties.

Surveys designed to estimate the amount and type of accommodation required have been undertaken on behalf of the Regional Group Consultative Committees. In the South West Region, for example, the Committee concluded that there were sufficient hostel beds in the region to meet the demand for accommodation for homeless men discharged from prison, but there was a serious shortage of accommodation for ex-prisoners who required special help or treatment.[3] In the South East Region, Walmsley[4] advocated greater co-ordination in the provision of accommodation and the introduction of a system which, by ensuring that different types of hostels and lodging houses worked together, would meet the individual needs of homeless men more adequately.

The probation and after-care service is particularly concerned with the problem because of its position as the social work service to the courts: as such it is frequently called upon by the Bench to help offenders who have nowhere to sleep. The responsibility of the probation officer may cease with the provision of a bed for the night or it may be extended if the offender is placed on probation. In either circumstance the short-term provision of accommodation is seen by most probation officers as only a first step in what is frequently a long process of rehabilitation to a more settled way of life. Many homeless offenders fail to achieve it and remain homeless for long periods, returning to the courts again and again with a regularity which is depressing for all those involved.

This study aimed to examine samples of homeless offenders from Liverpool from the time of their appearance in court. The report describes these offenders at different points in the system; it analyses some aspects of the sentencing process and looks at the offenders' responses to the sentences passed. It describes the role of the probation officer in recommending for or against probation, and discusses his attempts to help homeless men placed under supervision. Where offenders were sent to prison reference is made to their ongoing problem of homelessness and the roles of the prison welfare officer and the probation officer. The report shows that those men with real problems of homelessness (as distinct

3

from those who, though listed as being of no fixed abode, have a home to return to) present continual difficulties to the sentencers, to the probation and after-care service and to the community because of the apparently intractable nature of their homelessness.

The report suggests that decision-making about homeless offenders tends to be ambivalent, and that the giving or withholding of help is largely unrelated either to the offenders' needs or to the likelihood of resolving their presenting or underlying problems. Thus the progress of homeless offenders through the penal system tends to reflect a conflict between the desire to resolve the problem of homelessness and the awareness of most participants that such an objective is probably unattainable. The result is that decisions are often taken hesitantly in the full knowledge that the offenders will very likely continue to be in need and will appear again before the court and on the doorstep of the probation and after-care service in due course.

SECTION II

The Study and the Samples

The study was begun following discussions between the Liverpool Probation and After-Care Service, the North-West Regional Group Consultative Committee, and the Home Office Research Unit. Work began in March 1969 and the survey was undertaken as a joint project between the Liverpool Probation and After-Care Service and the Research Unit. The aims of the research were:

(i) to describe accurately the flow of samples of homeless offenders from Liverpool through the penal system with particular reference to the part played in their treatment by the probation and after-care service; and

(ii) to explore ways in which the treatment available to homeless offenders in the community might be improved.

It was apparent that the probation and after-care service could become involved at three major stages in the passage of homeless offenders through the penal process. These were before sentence, after sentence, and following release from institutions. At the time of an offender's appearance in court the service might well be asked to provide a social enquiry report. After sentence the service could be required to provide supervision under a probation order, or welfare facilities for an offender sent to prison. On release from prison, the service might be involved in the provision of statutory or voluntary after-care.

It was hoped that a study of the circumstances of selected samples of homeless offenders at these three stages would highlight the problems which related specifically to homelessness as opposed to the many other problems which most convicted men share. To achieve this two samples of homeless male offenders were taken: the first from men appearing before the courts, and the second from men receiving after-care following their release from prison.

In addition to isolating the particular problem of homelessness shared by all the men in these two samples, it was thought to be important to try to determine differences (if any) between their treatment and prognosis and those of other offenders who were the responsibility of the probation and after-care service. For this purpose of comparison samples were taken of offenders who were not homeless.

Details of the five samples selected for the study are given below. The first two described may be seen as the main samples about which the greatest amount of information was collected and upon which the major findings of the research rest. The three others were taken for the purpose of comparison mentioned in the preceding paragraph.

Sample 1–153 men

All the men appearing before the courts in Liverpool between 6 July 1967 and 31 July 1969 who were: (a) classified by the police as being of no fixed abode and

(b) remanded for a social enquiry report. Originally, 176 men satisfied both requirements, but 23 were subsequently excluded from the sample because 11 were found on enquiry to have settled accommodation which they had concealed from the police, and 12 social enquiry reports (upon which part of the research would be based) could not be traced.

For each case a copy of the social enquiry report was obtained and a content analysis was undertaken. After sentence all the cases were followed up for a period of 12 months. Where the offenders remained in contact with the probation and after-care service (e.g. by being placed on probation or being seen by a welfare officer in prison) copies of the officers' records were obtained and details recorded on analysis sheets. Further convictions during the follow-up period were recorded. The analysis sheets used for this sample are shown in Appendix I.

Sample 2—119 men

All the homeless men attending at the Liverpool After-Care Unit between 1 July and 31 December 1969 who were registered as new cases during that period. Cases were counted as 'new' if they had either not previously been to the Unit, or had not attended during the preceding 12 months.

The criteria used for classifying homelessness were developed with the co-operation of the officers at the Unit. A man was allocated to the homeless category by the officer who first interviewed him if either: (a) on the day he attended he had nowhere to sleep that night; or (b) after interviewing him the officer came to the conclusion that he had an established pattern of homelessness in his background. All the officers understood that an established pattern of homelessness implied that for at least 12 months before attending the Unit a man had lived entirely in common lodging houses, hostels, or other unstable accommodation of a similar nature, and had been moving about from place to place.

In respect of each homeless case the officer completed a schedule within one week of the man's first visit to the Unit, and all the cases were followed up for a period of 12 months from the date of first attendance. For the follow-up an analysis was made of the officers' records, and any further convictions were recorded. The schedule and analysis sheets used for this sample are shown in Appendix II.

Seventy-seven cases taken at random from this sample were the subjects of structured discussions between the supervising officer and the research worker in which an attempt was made (described in Section VI of this report) to assess the officers' attitudes to the homeless men.

Sample 3—72 men

All the men attending as new cases (see definition for Sample 2 above) at the Liverpool After-Care Unit between 1 July and 31 December 1969 who, at the time of their first visit, were in settled accommodation. This sample included all the men attending during the period who failed to meet the criteria of homelessness described for Sample 2. There were 90 such cases registered at the Unit during the period, but 11 were excluded because no record of contact had been kept, and a further 7 were excluded because the officers' records could not be traced. The information collected about these men was restricted to a content analysis of the supervising officers' records, and the recording of further convictions during a period of 12 months from the date of first contact. The analysis sheet used for the officers' records was identical with that employed for the homeless cases and is shown in Appendix II.

Sample 4—70 men

All the men who were registered as new cases by the whole of the Liverpool Probation and After-Care Service during the month of October 1969. Men were included in this sample if they came under the supervision of a Liverpool officer during that month, either by being placed on probation or by being released from a borstal or detention centre under licence. The only items of information recorded about these cases were age, criminal history and reconvictions during a period of 12 months from the dates of their first contacts. Additionally, the same structured discussion described under Sample 2 took place between the supervising officer and the research worker in respect of each case.

Sample 5—50 men

From 140 persons (excluding motoring offenders) who were fined at the Liverpool City Magistrates' Courts during the week commencing 22 April 1968, a sample was taken at random. The only information recorded for this sample was whether or not the fines were paid during a follow-up period of nine months, in order that this might be compared with the proportion of homeless men who paid their fines.

Discussions with probation officers

In addition to the structured discussions about individual cases mentioned under Samples 2 and 4, the research worker met each of the 10 senior probation officers who were in post in Liverpool at the time of the survey and sought their views about the problems of homeless offenders. These talks lasted between one and two hours and were open-ended, except that the researcher did ask each senior six specific questions. Similar discussions were held with all the officers and the senior at the After-Care Unit.

Limitations of the samples and methodology

The samples taken enable homeless offenders to be described in a number of circumstances, and to be compared with other offenders who, although similar in many respects, were not homeless at the time of the study. It is important to bear in mind, however, that the sampling was restricted to offenders in Liverpool,

and whilst some of the problems and situations described may well apply elsewhere, this will not be true of them all. There is no reason to suspect, however,
that there are great differences between areas. In fact, in an earlier study of
after-care units by Silberman & Chapman[5] samples were collected in Liverpool,
London and Manchester, and many of the men included in that study were
homeless, especially in London and Manchester, where officers dealt almost
exclusively with homeless voluntary after-care clients. It was borne in mind then
that the impressionistic account of the London unit might not apply to the
other places, but the report tried '. . . to analyse the problems faced by the unit
as well as describe its operation. In so far as these problems can be deduced
from the statistics, they may be expected to be common to the other units which
operate like Borough High Street (London) and which share with it, for example,
the characteristic of short contact with clients. Certainly the problems outlined
here seemed familiar to the probation officers at the other units and to the
research worker connected with them'. The general picture presented by the
clients of the after-care units seemed the same for all three places.

The methods used also had limitations which must be mentioned. The main
sources of information for the present study were probation officers' records
and social enquiry reports. Extracting particular items from records is well
known to be difficult since the absence of items of information may mean either
that the information is not available or that it is available but the officer has
failed to record it. Because of this a number of items from both social enquiry
reports and officers' records were excluded from the analysis. For example, it was
found that details of the offender's childhood were mentioned in some social
enquiry reports and some case records, but this was by no means consistent.
There were other items treated in a similar way such as factors which precipitated
the offender's homelessness.

Although there are these evident limitations, care was taken to ensure that any
items used were reliable and could be accurately measured for most cases.
Where particular items had been finally included in the analysis but there was
some doubt about their accuracy for a few cases, these cases were excluded from
the specific tables as will become apparent later on in the report.

SECTION III

Homeless Offenders before the Courts

This section deals with the group of offenders described in Section II as Sample 1. The sample was restricted to homeless men remanded for a social enquiry report by a Liverpool court during a two year period. These constituted a relatively small proportion of the total number of social enquiry reports. During 1968, for example, 2,614 social enquiry reports were prepared for the courts in Liverpool and of these only 72 (3%) related to homeless men. Although few in number, however, these men are an important minority because of the multiple problems they present.

Both magistrates and probation officers recognise an established pattern of homelessness in an offender's background as being a considerable impediment to the success of any form of penal treatment. The data do not enable an estimate to be made of the number of men, either nationally or in Liverpool, who are homeless when convicted, but the impression gained from discussions with probation officers and workers in other social agencies is that there has been an increase during the last five years. Urban renewal with the consequent demolition of cheap lodging houses in city centres was often quoted as being a source of increasing instability among men who have no families.

Types of homelessness

All the 153 men in this sample were homeless when they appeared before the courts, but it soon became apparent that there were various types of homelessness. At one end of the scale there were men who had been sleeping rough for a night or two following a quarrel at home, but would be able to return to their homes after sentence; whilst at the other end there were men who had lived the lives of vagrants for years and would probably continue to do so. Between these extremes were men who could be described as being at risk of becoming homeless. Whilst they frequently had accommodation, it was of such an unstable nature (e.g. lodgings) that even relatively small alterations in their circumstances could lead to their losing it. From a careful study of the social enquiry reports, three types of homelessness were defined as follows:

Vagrant. Men living a vagrant, tramp-like existence, frequently sleeping rough. Their accommodation was restricted to reception centres, common lodging houses and low grade hostels. Their problem of homelessness was long-standing.

At risk. Men at risk of becoming homeless. They usually had accommodation but it was not permanent, and they had no home to fall back on if for some reason their accommodation was lost (e.g. as a result of unemployment). As a consequence they occasionally slept rough.

9

Transient. Men whose homelessness was short-term and who had a home to
return to.

A few of the men did not fall into any of the three types, but most did; 36 (24%)
were classified as 'vagrant', 87 (57%) as 'at risk', while 20 (13%) were considered
'transient': 10 men could not be classified.

Characteristics of the homeless men

Most of the offenders in Sample 1 were adults and just over half (51%) were
30 years of age or older (Table 1).

Table 1

Homeless offenders before the courts: age distribution

Ages	Number of Men
Under 21	32 (21%)
21 but under 30	43 (28%)
30 but under 40	37 (24%)
40 and over	41 (27%)
Total	153 (100%)
Mean: 32·5 years	Range: 16–88 years

Despite their mature years, 106 (69%) of the men were single. Only 11 (7%) were
married or cohabiting, 4 (3%) were widowed, and 32 (21%) were separated or
divorced. It was clear from the social enquiry reports that, for many men, not
marrying or breakdown of marriage was only a reflection of their social incom-
petence and failure to lead a settled life.

Table 2 indicates the offences for which the men were convicted. An examination
of the reports shows that very few of the offences were serious: most were trivial

Table 2

Homeless offenders before the courts: the offences

Offences	Number of Men
Larceny/Receiving	66 (43%)
Fraud	26 (17%)
Break and enter	21 (14%)
Sexual offence	6 (4%)
Violence	5 (3%)
Other	29 (19%)
Total	153 (100%)

10

and could be seen more as a nuisance than as a threat to the community. Of the 66 offences of larceny or receiving, it was possible to discover the value involved in 41 of the cases; for 30 of them the amounts were less than £10. All but two of the 26 offences in the fraud group consisted of obtaining or attempting to obtain public funds to which the offender was not entitled.

Recommendations and sentences

Because of the mainly trivial nature of the offences and the clear inadequacy of many of these offenders, the courts were often at a loss to know what course to take. At a time when prison sentences must be used selectively, it is a consideration that men such as these are not dangerous or violent nor do they constitute a major threat to private or public property. Accordingly, in asking for a social enquiry report, the court is clearly anxious to act on a recommendation for probation if it seems at all possible that the offender will respond. However, only 29% of the men were recommended by probation officers as suitable for probation; they classed 57% as unsuitable, and made no recommendations about the remaining 14%.

Only 8 of the 44 men recommended for probation were not so dealt with by the court. 33% of the 153 men in the sample were put on probation; 27% were sentenced to custody in prison or elsewhere; 12% were fined; and 28% were conditionally discharged, given a suspended sentence or otherwise disposed of.

Table 3

Probation officers' recommendations compared with sentences imposed

Sentences Imposed	Recommendations		
	For Probation	Against Probation	Total
Probation	36 (82%)	10 (11%)	46
Other	8 (18%)	77 (89%)	85
Total	44 (100%)	87 (100%)	131
$\chi^2 = 63 \cdot 42$	df$=1$	$p < \cdot 001$	

It was clear from the reports that the probation officers were much concerned about the problem of homelessness and particularly the effect this might have during a period of probation. In many reports the offender's nomadic way of life was stressed as a primary reason for reaching the conclusion (often firmly expressed) that supervision in the community would be unsuitable. The following case example illustrates the point.

The offender was 49 years of age and single. His parents separated when he was a child and he was brought up in a children's home. He served for six years in the army during the war and after discharge he worked for a short time as a coal porter. For the 20 years prior to the sentence he had lived the life of a tramp, travelling from place to place all over the country. Occasionally he had worked as a kitchen porter, but for most of the time he was unemployed and when he appeared in court he had not worked for a year. The probation officer described him as a timid, rootless, friendless man who was inadequate and inarticulate and seemed much older than his years: his problems were deep-seated, stemming from his earliest experiences. Because he intended to move on and seldom stayed in one place for more than three weeks '. . . probation does not appear likely to help with either the present problems or the underlying reasons for them'.

This is one of many similar cases and because of the difficulties presented to the probation and after-care service by offenders who roam the country, it might be expected that there would be a close relationship between the seriousness of the offender's problem of homelessness and the recommendation made to the court. However, the types of homelessness ('vagrant', 'at risk' and 'transient') described in the reports were not associated with the recommendations made, and, although fewer men of the 'vagrant' type (those whose problem of homelessness was greatest) were recommended for probation, the differences between this group and the other two were not significant.

Moreover, as might have been expected from the close agreement between recommendations and sentences, it was found that the courts were no more influenced than were probation officers by the offenders' types of homelessness, although amongst the transient men only one was given a custodial sentence whilst 10 were placed on probation.

The only item consistently mentioned in the reports which was associated both with recommendation and sentence was the offenders' intentions for the future. Men who said that they intended to change or settle down, or those who indicated that they would co-operate with the probation officer, were much more likely to be recommended for probation and subsequently to be placed on probation. Table 4 compares the officers' recommendations with a positive indication from the offender that he would co-operate or change. Amongst those offenders who were recommended for probation 68% had expressed an intention to co-operate or change, whilst amongst those where the recommendation was against probation only 16% had expressed this intention.

It is consistent with much casework theory that for treatment to be a success, clients should have some insight into their problems or at least an awareness of a need for help. It seems likely that as caseworkers the probation officers were influenced by this concept and saw evidence of insight in the men's desire to change. In turn the courts were influenced by the officers' opinions, but unfortunately those factors were not associated with the successful outcome of penal treatment. When reconviction was taken as a measure of success, and the offenders were compared in terms of whether or not they had expressed an inten-

12

Table 4

Probation officers' recommendations compared with a positive indication to co-operate or change

Positive Indication	Recommendations	
	For Probation	Against Probation
Present	30 (68%)	14 (16%)
Absent	14 (32%)	73 (84%)
Total	44 (100%)	87 (100%)
$\chi^2 = 35\cdot54$	df=1	p<·001

tion of co-operating or changing, significant differences were not found (Table 5). Table 5 combines data on all forms of non-custodial sentences. There were significant differences in reconviction rates between the two sentence-groups 'probation' and 'other sentences'. Their combination in Table 5, however, is permissible because when they were analysed separately for the present comparison of positive indication with recommendation they did not differ significantly.

Table 5

A positive indication to co-operate or change compared with reconviction within twelve months

Reconviction	Positive Indication		
	Present	Absent	Total
Yes	19 (44%)	35 (55%)	54
No	24 (56%)	29 (45%)	53
Total	43 (100%)	64 (100%)	107
$\chi^2 = 1\cdot13$	df=1	Not significant	

It was thought that the three types of homelessness, identified from the descriptions of the men's circumstances contained in the reports, would reflect fairly accurately the offenders' general pattern of life, and that this in turn might provide an indication of their future conduct. It was hypothesised that the men at greatest risk of being convicted again would be those with the most serious problem of homelessness ('vagrant' type), whilst those men with a home to return to ('transient' type) would be much less likely to be reconvicted: the men in the 'at risk' type would occupy a middle position being less prone to reconviction than the 'vagrant', but at greater risk than the 'transient'. Table 6 shows

13

that this proved to be the case. 83% of the men in the 'vagrant' type were reconvicted within 12 months, compared with 43% for the 'at risk' and 32% for the 'transient'.

Table 6

Types of homelessness compared with reconviction within twelve months

Reconviction	Types of Homelessness			
	Vagrant	At Risk	Transient	Total
Yes	19 (83%)	26 (43%)	6 (32%)	51
No	4 (17%)	35 (57%)	13 (68%)	52
Total	23 (100%)	61 (100%)	19 (100%)	103

$\chi^2 = 13 \cdot 68$ df $=2$ p $< \cdot 01$

It seems that both probation officers and courts, anxious as they were to offer the help of supervision to men who might benefit from it, were misled by men whose apparent willingness to co-operate was not accompanied by the ability to do so. A man who has lived the life of a tramp for many years is unlikely to find it easy to change even if he wishes to do so, and his difficulties will be increased by his lack of resources. Thus it is not surprising that the more objective measure (the assessment of homelessness) was found to be associated with outcome rather than the assessment of the offender's attitude.

This argument would be considerably weakened if it were shown that the two items (type of homelessness and offender's intention) overlapped, or in other words if a significant proportion of offenders expressing a positive indication was found to be in a particular type of homelessness. Table 7 shows that this

Table 7

**Types of homelessness compared with recommendations
and a positive indication to co-operate or change**

Recommendation/ Positive Indication*	Types of Homelessness			
	Vagrant	At Risk	Transient	Total
For Probation/Present	6 (23%)	18 (30%)	3 (43%)	27
Against Probation/Absent	20 (77%)	43 (70%)	4 (57%)	67
Total	26 (100%)	61 (100%)	7 (100%)	94

$\chi^2 = 1 \cdot 12$ df $=2$ Not significant

* The figures are from the extreme groups in Table 4 (against probation/absent and for probation/present).

was not so. The two extreme groups were taken: those men for whom there was a recommendation for probation and who had expressed a positive indication; and those men for whom a recommendation against probation had been made and who had not said that they would co-operate. These groups are compared with types of homelessness and the differences are not significant.

It appears, therefore, that the types of homelessness, identified from the descriptions in the social enquiry reports, do reflect accurately the reality of offenders' situations and, so far as homelessness is concerned, their way of life.

15

SECTION IV

Homeless Offenders after Sentence

An attempt was made to follow-up all the men in Sample 1 for a period of 12 months after their court appearance, and wherever possible particular attention was given to their problem of homelessness. It has been shown that in the bulk of cases probation was considered unsuitable, and probation orders were made for only a third of the sample. 27% of the men were sent to prison or given other custodial sentences, and the remainder (40%) were released to the community without supervision: 24 of these men were given suspended prison sentences, 19 were conditionally discharged or bound over, and 18 were fined.

Homeless men released to the community without supervision

The men whose progress after sentence was most difficult to trace were those who were given suspended sentences, conditionally discharged or bound over. Searches were made of the central index kept by the Liverpool Probation and After-Care Service, the index maintained at the Liverpool After-Care Unit, and the daily diary kept at the courts by the duty probation officers. In addition, with the exception of three officers who had left the area, the officer who had undertaken the social enquiry for the court was asked in every case whether or not he had seen the offender again after sentence. The aim was to discover if these men, generally considered unsuitable for probation, had nevertheless been seen again by probation officers following their court appearance, and been given voluntary assistance. Only nine of the 43 men (21%) could be found to have had further contact with a probation officer, and only three of these had been given any practical assistance: one man was taken to a hostel by the officer and was supervised on a voluntary basis for three weeks, and the two others were given vouchers for hostel accommodation.

Homeless men who were fined

Eighteen of the homeless men (12%) were fined, and the amounts ranged from £5 to £208.* Six months after the fines were imposed a check showed that only three men had paid the full amount. One man had been sent to prison for non-payment, another had been deported, and for the remaining men warrants had been issued but not served. All four men for whom money payment supervision orders had been made when the fines were imposed failed to pay any money: each offender had disappeared on leaving the court and had not been in touch with the supervising officer before a warrant was issued. In discussion, the supervising officers made it clear that they considered money payment supervision ineffective for the majority of homeless offenders.

Because the proportion of homeless offenders who paid their fines was so low, it was decided to compare them with other offenders who were fined but were in

---

* Where compensation was ordered in addition to a fine, the amount was added to the total.

no other way connected with the study. Excluding motoring offenders, 140 persons were fined at the Liverpool City Magistrates' Courts during the week commencing 22 April 1968. From these offenders a random sample of 50 was taken (Sample 5 in Section II) and a check was made at the end of six months to determine how many had paid. 62% of the sample had paid their fines compared with 17% of the homeless offenders. The follow-up was then extended for a further three months: at the end of this time (nine months) 78% of the offenders in the random sample had paid, but the same check on the homeless men showed no increase in the proportion who paid the fines.

It appears that the disorganised way of life of the homeless men prevented them from paying their fines, and it was this that the money payment supervision officers suggested as the cause of their failure rather than any wilful determination not to pay.

Homeless men on probation

The 50 men who were placed on probation (33% of the sample) were followed up for 12 months and the probation officers' records for that period were studied in each case. Some of the men returned to their homes after being placed under supervision (22%), others settled in relatively stable accommodation (18%), but the majority remained homeless (68%).

When the original types of homelessness were compared with the proportions of probationers who remained homeless during the follow-up period (Table 8) it became clear that men with a long history of having nowhere to live ('vagrant') were much less likely to achieve a settled way of life than men in the other types.

Table 8

Types of homelessness compared with probationers' accommodation during the twelve months' follow-up period

Accommodation	Types of Homelessness			
	Vagrant	At Risk	Transient	Total
Remained homeless	13 (93%)	14 (56%)	3 (30%)	30
Settled in accommodation	1 (7%)	11 (44%)	7 (70%)	19
Total	14 (100%)	25 (100%)	10 (100%)	49

$$\chi^2 = 10\cdot30 \qquad df = 2 \qquad p < \cdot01$$

Probation officers often spent a good deal of time in attempting to assist men to find and keep a place to live, but in many instances these efforts were not matched by those of the clients.

17

The accommodation that probation officers can use for offenders is frequently restricted to hostels and the records showed that many of the men in the sample did not like them. The following case example illustrates some of the difficulties officers encountered.

CASE EXAMPLE

The offender was 69 years of age and had been a widower for 15 years. He had no children. He was brought up in an orphanage and had a long record of petty crime beginning in childhood. He had served many prison sentences including eight years preventive detention. He had roamed the country for the greater part of his life, taking casual employment as a labourer. The offence for which he was placed on probation for two years was stealing £5 from a fellow resident at a hostel for old people run by a religious organisation. In his report the probation officer recommended probation, saying that the offender claimed that he could not settle down in a religious atmosphere, but would do so if he could be found accommodation elsewhere. After the court appearance the officer took the probationer to hostel accommodation previously arranged for him and introduced him to the warden. During the following three weeks the officer visited the probationer at the hostel on three occasions, arranged for his pension book to be retrieved from his former accommodation, and tried to obtain some new clothing for him. The probationer complained to the officer about the hostel: he felt that he was a cut above the other residents, and the beds were very uncomfortable. At the beginning of the fourth week, the officer heard that the probationer had left the hostel and gone to Leicester. Before the officer could arrange for a probation officer there to pay the probationer's fare back to Liverpool, he had been arrested for stealing cigarettes and chocolate worth less than £1. Subsequently he was sentenced to seven days' imprisonment for the offence for which he had been placed on probation, and for the fresh offence a new probation order was made for three years. During the next twelve months the offender appeared in court on five occasions charged with stealing. He was conditionally discharged twice, absolutely discharged once, and sentenced to two terms of seven days' imprisonment.

Study of the probation officers' records showed that in just under half the cases (46%) the officer took some action to help the probationer resolve his problem of homelessness. This took the form of arranging hostel places, giving vouchers for accommodation, and in some instances (as in the case example quoted above) taking men to hostels and seeing them settled in. A number of men moved about a good deal during the follow-up period and were assisted by their probation officers with somewhere to stay on more than one occasion. The amount of involvement officers had in their clients' homelessness, and whether or not they took action to help resolve it, was found to be associated with the seriousness of the problem at the beginning of the order. Men for whom the problem was greatest ('vagrant') were much more

18

likely to be assisted than those for whom the problem was less acute ('at risk' and 'transient'). Table 9 shows the proportions of men in each of the three homelessness types who were assisted by probation officers to find somewhere to live.

Table 9

Types of homelessness compared with assistance given to probationers to find accommodation during the twelve months' follow-up period

Assisted to Find Accommodation	Types of Homelessness			
	Vagrant	At Risk	Transient	Total
Yes	11 (79%)	10 (40%)	2 (20%)	23
No	3 (21%)	15 (60%)	8 (80%)	26
Total	14 (100%)	25 (100%)	10 (100%)	49

$\chi^2 = 9{\cdot}00$ $df = 2$ $p < {\cdot}02$

Table 10 shows that among those probationers who were given assistance in finding accommodation a significantly greater proportion remained homeless than was the case among those who were not assisted.

Table 10

Help in finding accommodation or not compared with probationers' accommodation during the twelve months' follow-up period

Accommodation	Assisted to Find Accommodation		
	Yes	No	Total
Remained homeless	18 (78%)	12 (44%)	30
Settled in accommodation	5 (22%)	15 (56%)	20
Total	23 (100%)	27 (100%)	50

$\chi^2 = 5{\cdot}92$ $df = 1$ $p < {\cdot}02$

It has been shown (Table 9) that the probation officers' aid in finding accommodation was given selectively: the men whose need was greatest ('vagrant') were much more likely to receive help than the remainder, although success in settling men in accommodation was limited to five cases (20%). The examination of the probation officers' records showed that the help given was generally geared to short-term aid and frequently the probationer moved on or lost his

19

accommodation before anything more constructive could be done to help him*. For the sample as a whole the expression of a positive indication to co-operate or change was not significantly associated with an improved prognosis in terms of reconviction (Table 5). Probation officers were, however, more likely to recommend probation for men who expressed a positive indication (Table 4). Although the chances of reconviction for these men were not lessened, it might be thought that they would be more likely to settle down in accommodation. However, those men who expressed a positive indication before being placed on probation were no more likely to settle into accommodation than were the men who did not indicate a willingness to co-operate.

Again, despite the support of probation supervision, it appears that a long record of homelessness was strongly related to the likelihood of continuing difficulties (Table 8); and although the offenders' professed intention of changing influenced the probation officers in their recommendations, it was unrelated to the outcome of supervision in terms of remaining homeless. The prognosis depended essentially on the social circumstances prevailing at the beginning of supervision, and there was little to suggest that the client's determination to change or the probation officer's efforts to help him affected the position at all.

Homeless men in hospital, borstal and detention centre

Five men (3% of the whole sample) had histories of mental illness and were sent to psychiatric hospitals. One man had absconded from a psychiatric hospital before committing the latest offence. At the end of the 12 months' follow-up period three men were still in hospital as informal patients and two men had been discharged: one of them had a home in Scotland and when he recovered he returned there; no arrangements were made for accommodation of the other man on discharge and within a month he was admitted to a hospital in another town.

Four men were sent for borstal training and four to a detention centre. These men (3% of the whole sample) may be considered together. Two were still in custody at the end of the follow-up period, and two others were deported immediately following their release. For the remaining four the supervising probation officers' records were studied. Each of the men was visited before release by the probation officer responsible for after-care supervision and arrangements were made for their accommodation. Two men returned to their parents' home and settled there; but the other two (who were placed in hostels) continued to move from place to place and one of them disappeared, despite considerable efforts on the part of the officer to help him settle down.

---

* An attempt was made to inter-relate type of homelessness, assistance given, and the proportion of men who remained homeless, but the numbers in each cell were too small to enable any firm conclusions to be drawn. There was, however, no indication that the giving of assistance reduced the level of homelessness in any of the three groups—'vagrant', 'at risk' or 'transient'.

Numbers here are, of course, far too small for firm conclusions to be drawn, but it is perhaps worth noting that a careful examination of the available case records showed that performance after release was worse for those men who, at the time of sentence, had the more serious problem of homelessness.

Homeless men sentenced to imprisonment

Twenty-nine men were sent to prison. Eleven of them were sentenced to terms which precluded their being followed up during the period of the survey, and one man was deported. For 14 of the remaining 17 it was possible to trace the welfare or probation officers' records, but, because of the different lengths of sentence and variations in officers' record-keeping practices, only minimum information about homelessness was available. Some action was taken to resolve the problem for eight men, but only one man actually had accommodation arranged for him before discharge and there was no evidence that any assistance was given to help the other seven men find somewhere to live. This seemed to be due in part to the men's limited expectations of the welfare service (most of the problems that they brought were of an immediate practical nature), and in part to the belief of some of them that they would be able to find a place to live without any direct assistance.

SECTION V

Homeless Offenders on Release from Prison

The Liverpool After-Care Unit

A number of probation and after-care areas provide for men released from prison to be supervised at after-care units in which the officers specialise almost exclusively in voluntary and statutory after-care. The Liverpool Probation and After-Care Service set up its After-Care Unit in 1952. Initially, it dealt only with young men released from borstal training, but in 1966 it expanded its function to cater for the bulk of after-care cases in the city.

At the time of the survey a staff of six probation officers and one senior was employed. The officers' caseloads were composed of pre-release voluntary cases, ex-prisoners attending for voluntary after-care, parole and other statutory supervision, and a few borstal after-care and probation cases. Each of the officers was responsible for an area of the city, and any requests for pre-release work were allocated to the officer responsible for the area in which the prisoner's family lived.

Where information about homeless men was available before their release from prison, cases were allocated to officers by the senior, who took account of such items as the size of officers' caseloads, and whether or not a man had been known to a particular officer in the past. Most homeless men, however, arrived at the Unit without any previous arrangement having been made, and were generally retained on the caseload of the officer who was on duty on that day.

In order to study the problems which homeless ex-prisoners produced for the probation and after-care service, a sample (Sample 2 described in Section II) of 119 homeless men attending at the Liverpool After-Care Unit between 1 July and 31 December 1969 was collected and studied.

To put the homeless after-care cases into the perspective of the work of the Unit as a whole, a sample was taken (Sample 3 described in Section II) of men who were in settled accommodation when they attended at the Unit as new cases between 1 July and 31 December 1969. Officers did not complete schedules for these 72 men, but a content analysis of the case records for a period of 6 months from the date of first contact was undertaken and reconvictions over a period of 12 months were recorded.

Patterns of referral to the After-Care Unit

69% of the homeless men in Sample 2 came to the Unit of their own accord, some having been given assistance there previously; and only 25% had been referred by prison welfare officers. Table 11 shows how all the homeless men were referred to the Unit, and compares them with those who were in settled accommodation (Sample 3).

Table 11

**Sources of referral to the After-Care Unit:
a comparison between homeless men and those in settled accommodation**

Source of Referral	Accommodation at time of First Visit to the Unit		
	Homeless	Settled Accommodation	Total
Self-referred	62 (57%)	29 (40%)	91
Prison welfare officer	27 (25%)	27 (38%)	54
Previously known (self-referred)	13 (12%)	15 (21%)	28
Other agency	7 (6%)	1 (1%)	8
Total	109 (100%)	72 (100%)	181

$$\chi^2 = 9\cdot44 \qquad df = 3 \qquad p < \cdot05$$

The difference in referral patterns is apparently explained by the fact that more men who were referred by a prison welfare officer were subject to statutory supervision, and the statutory cases were less likely to be homeless (Table 12). When the non-statutory cases were examined separately, no relationship was found between the source of referral and the probability of homelessness.

Table 12

**Type of supervision at the After-Care Unit:
a comparison between homeless men and those in settled accommodation**

Type of Supervision	Accommodation at time of First Visit to Unit		
	Homeless	Settled Accommodation	Total
Statutory	7 (6%)	21 (29%)	28
Voluntary	102 (94%)	51 (71%)	153
Total	109 (100%)	72 (100%)	181

$$\chi^2 = 19\cdot13 \qquad df = 1 \qquad p < \cdot001$$

It did not necessarily follow that a prisoner referred by a welfare officer would be in a better position at the beginning of after-care than a man who introduced himself to the Unit. The records showed in general, however, that more was known about men who were referred by a welfare officer, and frequently the probation officer was made aware of specific problems (such as the need for accommodation) in advance of the prisoner's release. There was evidence in the records that this enabled a certain amount of forward planning to be undertaken designed to help the man to settle down more quickly. In discussion, the probation officers were agreed that advance information about men whom they would be required

C—28

to supervise was of considerable help to them, and its absence, which occurred in the majority of cases, was a handicap. A similar pattern of inadequate referral was shown by Silberman and Chapman[6] in an earlier study of the After-Care Units in Liverpool, London and Manchester.

Characteristics of the homeless after-care cases

As was the case amongst the homeless appearing before the courts, nearly all the homeless clients attending at the Unit were over 21 years of age, and as Table 13 shows, 65% were over the age of 30. However, the ages of the homeless men were significantly different from those of the men who were in settled accommodation at the time of their first visit to the Unit. Table 13 shows that the proportions of men aged between 30 and 40 years were similar for the two groups, but a much larger proportion of men in settled accommodation was under 30 years of age, whilst for the homeless men the largest proportion was over 40 years. The homeless men, therefore, were significantly older than the others attending for after-care supervision and, it might be thought, more set in their socially disorganised way of life as a consequence.

Table 13

The ages of the homeless men compared with those of the men in settled accommodation

Ages	Accommodation at time of First Visit to the Unit		Total
	Homeless	Settled Accommodation	
Under 30	41 (35%)	53 (60%)	94
30 but under 40	29 (24%)	18 (20%)	47
40 and over	49 (41%)	18 (20%)	67
Total	119 (100%)	89 (100%)	208

$\chi^2 = 14\cdot43$ $df = 2$ $p < \cdot001$

Although the number of men receiving statutory or voluntary after-care supervision from the probation and after-care service has been increasing for some years, this work still forms only a small part of most officers' caseloads.* So that the homeless men being supervised at the After-Care Unit could be seen in the wider perspective of the more usual cases dealt with by probation officers, a sample of new cases was taken (Sample 4 described in Section II) comprising all the men who came under the supervision of officers in Liverpool during October 1969. These men had been placed on probation or released from a borstal or detention centre during that month and will from now on be referred to in the

* At the end of 1970, for example, the statutory and voluntary supervision of offenders released from prison comprised only 8% of probation officers' caseloads in England and Wales.[7]

report as the October probation cases. There was a great difference in age between these more usual clients of the probation and after-care service and the homeless men at the After-Care Unit. Table 14 compares the ages of the October probation cases with those of the homeless men, and whilst the bulk of the October probation cases (81%) were aged under 21 years, only a very small minority (3%) of the homeless men were in this age group.

Table 14

The ages of the homeless after-care cases compared with those of the October probation cases

Ages	Groups of Offenders		
	Homeless After-Care Cases	October Probation Cases	Total
Under 21	3 (3%)	57 (81%)	60
21 but under 30	38 (32%)	10 (14%)	48
30 but under 40	29 (24%)	3 (4%)	32
40 and over	49 (41%)	0 (00%)	49
Total	119 (100%)	70 (100%)	189

$$\chi^2 = 131 \cdot 17 \qquad df = 3 \qquad p < \cdot 001$$

This age difference between homeless prison after-care cases and most other clients of the probation and after-care service has implications for both the methods of treatment necessary for the homeless group and the attitudes of the officers who specialise in dealing with them at the Unit. This difference is examined later in the report.

The largest group of homeless men were single (58%), and only 6% were married. These figures are not significantly different from those reported for the court cases, and confirm the results in Section III.

Most of the homeless men were recidivists and 70% had been convicted on six or more earlier occasions, whilst only 17% had fewer than four previous convictions. In this respect these clients again differed greatly from the October probation cases, amongst whom only 12% had six or more previous convictions and 81% had been previously convicted on less than four occasions. Officers were able to make an assessment of the social life of 92 homeless men, and of these only 14% were said to mix mainly with non-criminals; 41% were described as lone wolves, and 45% mixed mainly with criminals. The large proportion of men associating with criminals can be seen in part as a reflection of the company available to them in their accommodation. Eighty-one men (68% of the sample) had somewhere to live when they attended at the Unit, and for 72 of these the supervising officers were able to give an indication of the criminal tendencies of other men sharing the accommodation. Criminality among the people with whom the client lived was marked in 83 % of cases, slight in 15 % and absent in only 1 %. The homeless men, therefore, can be seen as either social isolates or as mixing mainly with criminals. Few men enjoyed some social contacts but at the same time avoided criminals.

The problems of the homeless after-care cases

The problems which the men brought to the officers at the Unit give some indication of their way of life and of their expectations of the after-care service. In general, the men confined their requests for help to the immediate practical problems which were causing them most concern at the time of their visit, and there is virtually no evidence in the records to suggest that any approached the Unit with long-term support or help in mind. The problems which the men presented at their first visit to the Unit are shown in Table 15.

Table 15

The problems presented by homeless men

Presenting Problems	Number of Men
Accommodation	47 (43%)
Money	37 (34%)
Employment	30 (28%)
Clothing	27 (25%)
Other	14 (13%)
No information	5 (5%)

N=109 Some men presented more than one problem

The forms of immediate help the men were given reflect the requests they made, and Table 16 shows that the homeless men were most frequently referred to other agencies (usually the Supplementary Benefits Section of the Department of Health and Social Security or the then Department of Employment and Productivity) or were assisted directly in finding accommodation. 22% of the men were advised about employment prospects in the area, but for only 5% did officers intervene directly in finding work.

Significantly fewer of the men in settled accommodation (p < ·05) were given a grant of cash, and very many more of them (p < ·001) were either assisted to find employment or advised about employment prospects.

These differences can be seen as an indication of the greater pressure which the problem of homelessness brought both to the clients and to the officers trying to help them. With the homeless men the focus of attention and action was by necessity frequently on this basic problem; and other difficulties, such as lack of employment (only 3% of the homeless men were working when they first came to the Unit), were given a lower priority.

Table 16

Forms of help given at the After-Care Unit

Forms of Help Given	To the Homeless Men		To the Men in Settled Accommodation	
	Number of Men	%	Number of Men	%
Referred to other agency	44	(40%)	19	(26%)
Assistance in finding accommodation	43	(39%)	2*	(3%)
Cash grant	36	(33%)	14	(19%)
Advice about employment prospects	24	(22%)	34	(47%)
Assistance with practical problems	14	(13%)	26	(36%)
Clothing	19	(8%)	11	(15%)
Assistance in finding employment	5	(5%)	7	(10%)
Other material assistance	3	(3%)	0	(0%)
No action recorded	13	(12%)	8	(11%)
	N=109		N=72	

Some men were given more than one of the forms of help listed.
* These men wished to change their accommodation.

In addition to noting the immediate practical problems in the case records, officers completed for each case, a problem checklist. This list, of 10 personality items, was taken from a list of 61 personality and social problems devised by Folkard (and described by Simon [8]) as giving a measure of deviance.* Officers were asked to rate the severity of each problem on a five-point scale ranging from 'absent' to 'very severe'. Table 17 lists all the problems and the proportions of men rated on the five-point scale.

Thus, for each item, almost a third of the men were assessed as having the problem to a moderate degree. This may be due in part to difficulties in making assessments on the large number of men (41% of the whole sample) who were seen on only one occasion. This brief contact may also account for the large proportion of 'don't know' responses made to some items, and as a consequence the ratings as a whole should be treated with some caution.

It is worth noting, however, that where 'moderate' ratings were not given the tendency was to score items at the 'severe' end of the scale. This applied to all problems except 'anti-authority attitudes', 'callousness' and to a lesser extent 'anti-social attitudes', where the larger proportions were found at the 'mild' or 'absent' end of the scale. This may well reflect the officers' view, expressed in discussions with the researcher, that these homeless men could be seen as more inadequate than wilfully criminal, and as having characters which were typified

* The ratings on the problem checklist were converted into a 'deviance score' and this was found to be associated with reconviction. The higher the score the more likely it was that a man would be reconvicted (p < ·05). For a description of the deviance score and a comparison of the homeless men with a sample of probationers see Appendix III.

Table 17

Homeless men rated on the problem checklist

Problems	Very Severe	Severe	Moderate	Mild	Absent	N	Don't Know
	Ratings						
	%	%	%	%	%		
Little conscience	14	35	26	20	5	96	23
Drunkenness	23	19	26	16	16	80	39
Anti-authority attitudes	6	19	30	25	21	108	11
Dishonesty	19	34	32	13	2	108	11
Irresponsibility	15	43	30	11	1	105	14
Callousness	5	19	31	31	15	59	60
Delinquent tendencies	17	35	30	19	0	107	12
Untruthfulness	9	28	38	23	2	64	55
No loyalties	16	29	26	20	9	86	33
Anti-social attitudes	12	22	31	29	6	98	21

more by weakness than viciousness. In this the descriptions of many of the homeless men matched very closely those given in the social enquiry reports made on them when they were before the court.

The homeless men were also rated by the officers for mental and physical health and the presence of any physical disability. Where it was known that a client had been examined by a psychiatrist during the 12 months preceding his first visit to the Unit this was recorded, together with an assessment of the severity of the problem of mental illness. In respect of physical illness or disability the officers made all the assessments themselves. Table 18 gives the details.

Table 18

Mental and physical health of the homeless men

A. MENTAL HEALTH

Mental Illness a Problem?	Psychiatric Examination	No Psychiatric Examination	Total
	Number of Men	Number of Men	
Very much so	8	1	9 (8%)
Slightly	5	15	20 (17%)
Not at all	2	88	90 (76%)
Total	15	104	119 (100%)

B. PHYSICAL HEALTH

Physical Ill-health or Disability a Problem?	Number of Men
Very much so	7 (6%)
Slightly	14 (12%)
Not at all	98 (82%)
Total	119 (100%)

Probation officers are not, of course, qualified to make medical assessments and the opinions they gave, apart from those few cases where a psychiatric examination had been made, were the judgements of lay observers based on what the clients themselves reported and the officers could see during their interviews. Bearing these obvious limitations in mind, it can be noted that officers judged mental illness to be a severe problem in only 8% of the men, and physical illness or disability in only 6%.

So far as lay observers were concerned, therefore, these homeless men were in general reasonably fit both mentally and physically. Despite this, only four of them were actually in employment when they first called at the Unit and many of them had long histories of unemployment. Table 19 shows how the men's work records were assessed.

Table 19

The homeless men's employment records

Unsteady Work Record: A Problem in the Past	Number of Men
Very much so	75 (63%)
Slightly	33 (28%)
Not at all	9 (8%)
No information	2 (2%)
Total	119 (100%)

Almost two-thirds of the men were assessed as having very poor employment histories, and it was clear from the detailed study of the officers' records that almost all of these men had not worked in any regular way for many years, and the officers thought it unlikely that they would do so in the future. For 8% of the men officers found no evidence of an unsteady work record, and for nearly all the rest (28%) they said the problem was only slight.

These men with 'slight' or 'no' unsteady work records, representing just over one-third of the sample, were specially considered to determine whether they differed in any other ways from the remainder of the men. There were no differences in terms of age or of the number of problems presented when they first called at the Unit. In discussion* with the research workers, the officers did not assess the men as being better prospects for long-term casework treatment, or any less likely to be reconvicted. There were, however, importants ways in which they were different from the men whose employment records were poor. They had fewer previous convictions ($p < \cdot001$), they were rated as having fewer 'very severe' and 'severe' problems ($p < \cdot001$), and in the discussions officers classed fewer of them as 'hopeless' cases ($p < \cdot001$). In their degree of homeslessness they were also different. At the time of their first visit to the Unit they were less likely to have been sleeping rough or to have been in very unstable accommodation ($p < \cdot001$). Lack of somewhere to live in the past was less likely to have been a problem ($p < \cdot001$), and, in assessing their future accommodation prospects, officers were less likely to suggest that their problem of homelessness would continue ($p < \cdot001$).

The items on which these men differed from the remainder of the sample can be seen as inter-related in a practical way. Their ability to work could have been the key to their better accommodation in the past and present, or the fact that they had somewhere to live might have produced their better work records. From the data available it is impossible to suggest cause and effect, but the items mentioned, together with the men's relative lack of criminal sophistication, identified these men to the probation officers as a more hopeful group. They had not descended to a life of vagrancy and the officers thought that they might settle down. Despite these more hopeful signs, however, the officers' case records revealed that these men were not given any treatment different either in quantity or quality from that given to the remainder, and their reconviction rates did not differ significantly when they were compared with the rest of the sample.

The duration of after-care treatment

The study undertaken in 1966 by Silberman and Chapman [9] of the After-Care Units in London, Liverpool and Manchester showed that one of the characteristics of after-care treatment was its short-term nature. In the Liverpool Unit at that time 47% of the clients were seen on only one occasion. In the present study the finding was identical: when the two samples (the homeless men and the men in settled accommodation) were taken together, 47% of the men had called only once at the Unit.

There was no significant difference between the homeless men and the men in settled accommodation in the number of contacts they had with the Unit, but the homeless men stayed in touch with their probation officers for a shorter time. Table 20 compares the two groups and shows that whilst 29% of the men in settled accommodation stayed in contact for three months or longer, only 10% of the homeless men did so.

---

* For a description of these discussions, see Section VI.

Table 20

Length of contact with the After-Care Unit:
a comparison between homeless men and those in settled accommodation

Length of Contact	Accommodation		
	Homeless	Settled Accommodation	Total
Less than one month	82 (75%)	42 (58%)	124
One month but less than three months	16 (15%)	9 (13%)	25
Three months and longer	11 (10%)	21 (29%)	32
Total	109 (100%)	72 (100%)	181

$$\chi^2 = 10\cdot88 \qquad df = 2 \qquad p < \cdot 01$$

It is possible that the homeless men broke off contact sooner because their problems were satisfactorily resolved and they had no further need of assistance. The prognoses made by the probation officers, which are discussed later in this Section, make this unlikely, and it seems more probable that the homeless men kept in touch for shorter periods because of their unsettled way of living and their tendency to move on after a short time in one place. This latter view was also confirmed in the study of the officers' records: almost invariably in cases where contact was lost the client had been offered a further appointment which he had failed to keep.

Homelessness and reconviction

In completing the schedule for each of the homeless cases, officers were asked to assess the men's homelessness at three points in time: the past, the present, and the future. Table 21 shows the officers' assessments.

For men who had been known to officers in the past (12% of the cases) assessments of previous homelessness were based on factual information. In most cases, however, all the assessments, past, present and future, were founded on what the men told officers about themselves in interview and what the officers could observe. Again it should be noted that in 41% of cases there was only one interview, and as a consequence the assessments should be seen as only an approximate guide to the real state of affairs.

From Table 21 emerges the clear belief of the officers in the continuing nature of homelessness. The proportion of cases who in the past had a severe problem of homelessness is almost identical with the proportion who were seen as being likely to continue to be homeless in the future.

Unfortunately, it was not possible in the follow-up to test the accuracy of the officers' predictions. Only 10% of the men stayed in touch for longer than three

Table 21

Probation officers' assessments of homelessness at three points in time

A. THE PAST

Extent to which Unstable Accommodation was a Pattern in Men's Lives	Number of Men
Very much so	63 (53%)
Moderately	34 (29%)
Slightly	13 (11%)
Not at all	9 (8%)
Total	119 (100%)

B. THE PRESENT

Accommodation at the Time of First Visit to the Unit	Number of Men
Sleeping rough	24 (20%)
Very unstable	25 (21%)
Fairly unstable	32 (27%)
Fairly stable	25 (21%)
Very stable	13 (11%)
Total	119 (100%)

C. THE FUTURE

The Predicted Future Accommodation	Number of Men
Very unstable	62 (52%)
Fairly stable	48 (40%)
Very stable	9 (8%)
Total	119 (100%)

months, and it was impossible to discover what types of accommodation the men who disappeared went to. 73% of the men were reconvicted within 12 months, however, and whilst it cannot be assumed from this that most of them remained homeless, it is an indication that the criminal pattern of their lives stayed much the same.

Unlike the sample of homeless offenders appearing before the courts, the assessments of homelessness were not associated with reconviction. Men for whom the problem of homelessness was assessed as being least severe (in the past, present and future) were just as likely to be reconvicted as were those men for whom the problem was most acute. This might be thought surprising in view of the experience with the court cases, but the difference between the samples is probably due to differences in the methods of assessment. The men appearing before the courts were subject to detailed enquiries, whilst many of the men at the After-Care Unit were not. The assessments made of the degree of homelessness amongst the court cases, therefore, probably reflected much more accurately the reality of their situations.

A large proportion of the homeless men were reconvicted within 12 months of their first visit to the Unit, as Table 22 shows.

Table 22

Reconviction rates compared for the homeless after-care cases, the after-care cases in settled accommodation and the October probation cases

Reconvicted	After-Care		Probation	Total
	Homeless	Settled Accommodation	October Probation Cases	
Yes	80 (73%)	40 (51%)	21 (32%)	141
No	30 (27%)	39 (49%)	44 (68%)	113
	110 (100%)	79 (100%)	65 (100%)	254

$\chi^2 = 9 \cdot 68$ for Homeless *v.* Settled Accommodation cases (df=1 p<·005)
$\chi^2 = 27 \cdot 35$ for Homeless *v.* October Probation cases (df=1 p<·001)

The percentage of homeless men reconvicted was 73; compared with 51% for the men in settled accommodation, and 31% for the October probation cases. The figures for the homeless men are significantly different from either of the two other groups. These figures underline the size of the problem that homeless ex-prisoners present to probation officers attempting to aid their rehabilitation. The failure of after-care treatment to keep so many homeless men out of trouble with the police has a depressing effect on the probation officers concerned, and this is reinforced by the recurring failure of the men to settle into the accommodation arranged for them.

The overall picture of short-term contacts, lack of response to the immediate aid given, and the high incidence of reconviction is a gloomy one, and the implications for the methods of treatment employed and the attitudes of the officers dealing with homeless offenders are discussed in Section VI.

SECTION VI

Probation Officers' Attitudes towards Homeless Offenders

Homeless offenders before the courts

There were in Liverpool at the time of the study eight district probation and after-care offices, and a request from a court for a social enquiry report was dealt with by an officer for the district in which the offender lived. For homeless offenders the procedure was different. When the court asked for a report about an offender without an address, the senior probation officer serving the court allocated the enquiry to a district office on a rota basis; and an officer there undertook it.

As mentioned in Section III of this report, the number of homeless men for whom social enquiry reports were prepared represented only a very small proportion of the total enquiries that Liverpool officers undertook during the period of research. Nevertheless, it was suggested that these men were a significant minority because of the problems which they presented.

In order to explore some of the difficulties involved in making social enquiries about homeless offenders the researcher held a discussion with each of the ten senior probation officers then in post in Liverpool. The discussions, which lasted for between one and two hours, ranged quite widely over many aspects of homelessness and were completely open-ended. To give them a focus, however, six specific questions were put to each senior.

Detailed notes about the discussions were made immediately after they had taken place and the responses to the six questions were recorded. The questions were as follows:

1. In undertaking social enquiries are there any ways in which homeless men present more difficulties to the officer?
2. Do homeless offenders have more problems than other men for whom reports are prepared?
3. Disregarding any other problems which these offenders have, what difference (if any) does the presence of homelessness make to the officer undertaking the enquiry?
4. What resources are the probation officers in your district able to call upon to resolve an offender's problem of homelessness?
5. Are these resources (if any mentioned in response to question 4) adequate?
6. What additional local resources (if any) do you feel would be necessary to help homeless offenders adequately?

The discussions were of an exploratory nature, undertaken to gain insight into the difficulties officers encountered with homeless offenders about whom they had to make enquiries. It was also hoped that an indication would be gained of the feelings which officers have about homeless men. It cannot be assumed that this group of senior officers was representative of the probation and after-care service as a whole, or that their views coincided with those of the probation officers in their district offices. As a group, however, they held responsible positions and on those points where there was agreement between them they could well be seen as representing an important influence in the Liverpool Probation and After-Care Service at that time.

All the seniors were agreed (question 1) that homeless offenders, almost by definition, presented more difficulties than others to an officer making enquiries. The form which the difficulties took, however, varied considerably. A number of the seniors focussed their attention on the problem which the finding of suitable accommodation would pose for the officer, and it is perhaps interesting to note that here an assumption was made that a period of probation would be the outcome of the enquiry and the court appearance. Others asserted that home-less men presented more difficulties because the lack of somewhere to live often confused an otherwise clear situation. An offender, for example, who was thought suitable for probation in all other respects could, because of his lack of somewhere to live, raise doubts in an officer's mind about his real ability to respond to supervision and could as a consequence make the officer's decision about a recommendation much more difficult.

On question 2 views varied. One senior felt that homeless offenders did not have any more problems than the other men apart from their lack of a place to live: the nine other officers took the contrary view, but saw the forms of the problems variously. Several stressed the important part played by character disorders of homeless men and portrayed them as being very inadequate in personality. Weakness, retarded emotional development, and inability to form meaningful relationships were phrases which constantly recurred in the discussions. Home-lessness and a wandering way of life were seen as by-products of these under-lying disorders of personality development. Problems of a more practical nature were mentioned also, as shown in Table 23.

Table 23

Senior probation officers' assessments of homeless offenders' problems

Problems	Number of Senior Officers rating the Problem as Present in:		
	Most Cases	Many Cases	Few Cases
Poor work record	7	3	0
Poor management of money	8	2	0
Drink	5	4	1
Drugs	0	4	6
Poor personal appearance	9	1	0
Bed-wetting	4	4	2
Soiling	0	5	5

Number of senior officers = 10

The problems listed in Table 23 were mentioned by all the seniors in the discussions. Other problems, such as homosexuality, low intelligence, and mental and physical illness, were raised by only a few and were seen by them as being of only marginal importance.

Question 3 produced a unanimous response. Homelessness, it was said, always made a considerable difference to the officer and invariably produced more difficulties for him. Two seniors responded with the identical phrase '. . . the heart sinks when one hears it is another homeless enquiry'. The difficulties in finding suitable accommodation if the offender were to be released to the community were raised by all the seniors, and five stressed the problem for an officer in making a realistic recommendation.

All the seniors, in response to question 4, knew of at least one hostel to which homeless men could be referred. A recurrent difficulty, however, was that almost all the hostels and lodging houses were in or near the centre of the city and local resources were often completely inadequate (question 5).

Question 6 drew a range of responses. Only two seniors saw need for an increased number of hostel places, but all were agreed that there was a pressing need for an increase in the range of accommodation available. Homeless men, it was said, were not a homogeneous group and their needs differed greatly. Some could respond to a hostel regime, but others were in need of landlady-type digs, and some could be helped best by being placed with a family. Only one senior knew of a landlady to whom he could refer men, and these needed to be very carefully selected cases. No accommodation with families was available and, although the number of men suitable for this was thought to be small, its absence was described as a serious gap in the resources available.

The need to involve the local community in the provision of accommodation was emphasised by several seniors, but the attempts made to do so (for example, by advertising in the local paper) had all failed because of the poor response. One senior suggested that the reason for the failure was the fragmented nature of the attempts which had been made, and advocated the appointment of a full-time officer whose sole task would be to find and vet accommodation and keep an up-to-date record of whatever was available in the city. In this way a large part of the burden of finding, on an *ad hoc* basis, suitable places to live would be removed from the probation officers, who would thus be enabled to concentrate on clients' other problems.

In general, therefore, the ten seniors considered that the current situation was poor. Homeless offenders presented multiple problems and there was an acute shortage of appropriate resources to meet their needs.

Homeless offenders at the After-Care Unit

The discussions held with the officers at the After-Care Unit were focussed on the particular men whom they supervised. From the 119 homeless men in

36

Sample 2 (see Section II), 77 were taken at random, and for each case the researcher put five statements to the supervising officer, who allocated them to a 'true' or 'false' category. If an officer was at all doubtful about a statement being completely true it was recorded as false. The five statements and the officers' responses to them are shown in Table 24.

Table 24

Probation officers' responses to five statements about homeless after-care cases

Statement	Responses	
	'True'	'False'
1. I was able to form a good relationship with this man	46 (60%)	31 (40%)
2. I was able to help this man with some of his short-term problems	74 (96%)	3 (4%)
3. This man is likely to respond to long-term casework treatment	16 (20%)	61 (80%)
4. I found it impossible to like this man	9 (12%)	68 (88%)
5. This seems to be a hopeless case	37 (48%)	40 (52%)

N=77

It is not possible from the data available to show with any certainty the grounds upon which officers' responses to the five statements were based. There was, however, a good deal of consistency in their answers, and one example of this was that in no case did an officer answer true to both questions 1 and 4.

The responses recorded were examined in relation to each other and to other information collected, and a number of significant associations were found for statements 1, 3 and 5. Those men with whom the officers were able to form good relationships had fewer 'very severe' and 'severe' problems on the problem checklist ($p < .01$), were assessed as having better accommodation prospects in the future ($p < .01$), were thought to be more likely to respond to casework ($p < .01$), and were less likely to be assessed as 'hopeless' cases ($p < .01$). Those who were assessed as being likely to respond to casework were younger ($p < .05$). Those men who were assessed as 'hopeless' were found to be older ($p < .05$), have unsteady work records ($p < .001$), have worse accommodation in the past ($p < .05$), and a greater number of 'very severe' and 'severe' problems on the problem checklist ($p < .001$). None of the five statements was found to be significantly associated with either number of previous convictions or further convictions during the follow-up period.

The concept of hopelessness can be seen as being of central importance. The probation officers always considered this statement very carefully and particularly so before judging it to be true. One officer remarked that it really went against the grain to accept that some men were hopeless and could not be helped by treatment. Nevertheless, all the officers accepted that it was true for some of their clients and, as Table 24 shows, just under half the cases discussed were said to be hopeless.

It seems from the analysis that in reaching the conclusion that men were hopeless officers took into account the nature of a man's homelessness (i.e. how much of a problem it had been in the past), the magnitude of his other problems, and the difficulty the officer experienced in forming a working relationship. Where these items combined in a negative way a man was much more likely to be assessed as hopeless, and this group of hopeless men was seen as forming the hard core of homeless offenders who were virtually untreatable.

For the purposes of comparing the officers' attitudes towards their homeless clients with those of officers dealing with the more usual clients of the probation and after-care service, the five statements were put to the officers supervising the seventy October 1969 probation cases (Sample 4 in Section II). Table 25 shows the responses of both groups of officers and, where there were differences between them, the level of significance.

Table 25

Officers' responses to five statements:
a comparison between the homeless after-care cases and the
October probation cases

Statement	Percentage Answering 'True'		
	Homeless After-Care Cases %	October 1969 Probation Cases %	Significance Level
1. I was able to form a good relationship with this man	60	61	N.S.
2. I was able to help this man with some of his short-term problems	96	83	$p < \cdot 01$
3. This man is likely to respond to long-term casework treatment	21	56	$p < \cdot 001$
4. I found it impossible to like this man	12	1	$p < \cdot 02$
5. This seems to be a hopeless case	48	13	$p < \cdot 001$
N	77	70	

The proportions of men with whom officers were able to form a good relationship were virtually identical for the two groups, but for all the other statements the differences were large. Significantly fewer of the October probation cases were helped with short-term problems, but many more of them were seen as likely to respond to long-term casework treatment. Despite there being only a few homeless men who were found to be impossible to like, it was a significantly larger proportion than that found among the October probation cases, and this emphasises the difficulties encountered by officers dealing with homeless men.

Lastly, very many more of the homeless men were assessed as being 'hopeless' cases.

The difference in officers' attitudes suggests that the treatments they gave were also different. The view that long-term treatment was unsuitable for many of the homeless men was reinforced by the fact that 75% of them remained in contact for less than one month (see Table 20) and this in turn implied that if any work was to be done it had to be undertaken quickly. Inevitably this meant a focus on short-term, pressing difficulties, such as the provision of a bed for the night; and a neglect of underlying problems which might take much longer to resolve. Because of the failure of so many men to return, officers were largely unaware of the effects of the treatment which they had been able to give. In discussions, however, it was clear that from their experience they thought it unlikely that many men had been helped to settle down permanently or to keep out of further trouble. All the officers acknowledged that this conclusion had a depressing effect upon them and often led them to question the value of the type of treatment they were able to give within the framework of the limited resources available.

The officers' attitudes towards homeless clients and the feelings of frustration they experienced in dealing with them were accurately summarised in the words of one of them who said '. . . whilst I am always willing to go on trying with homeless men, I am glad for the sake of my morale that I also have other more hopeful cases to deal with'.

SECTION VII

Summary and Discussion

Summary of major findings

This research has attempted to trace the course of samples of homeless offenders through the penal system, to examine their problems, and to study the difficulties they create for the probation officers responsible for supervision. It has been shown that probation officers became involved at three stages in the penal process, and these are summarised below.

1. Homeless offenders before the courts

The first point of contact studied was when homeless offenders appeared in court, and probation officers were asked to make social enquiries. It was clear from the sample studied (153 men) and the discussions held with senior officers about homeless offenders in general, that officers found great difficulty in making realistic recommendations in their reports. The problem of homelessness, particularly if it was long-term, confused the situation. Although the offences which the men had committed were largely trivial, and although many of the men were in need of support if they were to remain in the community, the officers frequently recommended against probation. They did so in 57% of the cases and as a rule the reason given for the opinion that an offender was unsuitable for supervision was his wandering way of life, which would be a barrier against any ongoing work.

However, 29% of the sample were recommended for probation. A significant proportion of these offenders had told the officers that they would co-operate or settle down, and this, rather than the severity of the problem of homelessness, appeared to influence the officers to recommend probation. The offenders' intentions, however, were not associated with the outcome of treatment in terms of either remaining homeless or being reconvicted. It was the severity of the problem of homelessness which was associated with outcome, and it was the men for whom the problem was greatest who remained homeless and were reconvicted more frequently.

2. Homeless offenders after sentence

Little information was available about the 43 homeless offenders who were released by the court to the community without supervision, and it was not possible to discover whether or not they remained homeless. Nine of these men were seen by a probation officer after sentence, but only three were given any help to find accommodation. The accommodation to which the men who were fined went was unknown, but very few of them paid the sums that the court had ordered.

Follow-up information about the 29 men who were sent to prison was also scanty, but such as there was tended to suggest that where homelessness had been a serious problem it remained unresolved. In this respect they did not differ greatly from the 13 men who were sent to other forms of institutional treatment.

The largest amount of information about homeless offenders after sentence concerned the 50 men who were placed on probation. The probation officers concentrated their efforts on those men with the greatest problem of homelessness, but, despite this, most of them remained homeless during the follow-up period. The likelihood of remaining homeless was again related to the seriousness of the problem at the time of sentence and not to the intention to co-operate or settle down which some of the offenders had expressed.

3. **Homeless offenders on release from prison**

These 119 men, attending the Liverpool After-Care Unit, were supervised by officers who specialised in the after-care of ex-prisoners and who had large experience of dealing with homeless offenders. Because all the men had been to prison on at least one occasion they could be seen as a more homogeneous group than the homeless offenders before the courts (see paragraph 1 above). They presented multiple problems and many had been homeless for long periods. They were, however, dissimilar in some ways. Whilst 63% of the 119 men had poor work records, for example, and had not held a job for many years, the remainder were assessed by the officers as having had reasonable employment histories, and these men appeared to have more hopeful prospects in other ways as well.

It cannot be said that the picture of homeless ex-prisoners was anything but gloomy. Just under half of them were assessed as being 'hopeless' cases and few (21%) were thought likely to respond to long-term casework; but for 52% more of them officers believed that treatment was possible. However, officers stressed the lack of resources with which to meet the needs of the men whom they were required to supervise, and in 75% of the 119 cases contact was lost within one month.

Conclusions

The aims of the research (set out in Section II) were to describe the flow of samples of homeless offenders through the penal system in relation to the part which probation officers played in their treatment, and to explore ways in which treatment in the community might be improved. Whilst the first of these aims has been realised, it should be borne in mind that the nature of the study does not allow firm conclusions to be drawn about the second. Among the homeless men appearing before the courts for example, the finding that the offenders' intentions were related to the recommendations made and sentences imposed, but not to outcome, does not imply that if officers were to ignore intentions their assessments would be more accurate. Nevertheless, the findings do prompt certain speculations which, provided they are seen as such and not as firmly

41

proved evidence, could form the basis of hypotheses for subsequent research to test.

The two main samples, the court cases and the after-care cases, had certain features in common. These were their homelessness, the presence of multiple problems, and their lack of response to treatment in the community. These features may be considered in relation to assessment, treatment and resources. It was clear that officers in making assessments attached a lot of weight to homelessness as a problem. It was, for example, frequently mentioned in the social enquiry reports as being an impediment to treatment. It was not seen as a total barrier to treatment, however, as among the court cases some men in the vagrant type were recommended for probation, and among the after-care cases some men were seen as being suitable for long-term casework.

The assessments were not related to outcome, and this was true (among the homeless probationers) even when the officers made additional efforts to assist the men. It could be hypothesised that the assessments were inadequate because, although officers gave considerable weight to homelessness, they still failed to perceive the magnitude of the problem. In other words, where the problem of homelessness was most severe it was of central importance, and in the absence of its satisfactory resolution the men were almost certain to fail.

If the failure of so many cases was in fact due to faulty assessments of the importance of homelessness, the implication is that attempts to improve treatment must entail greater efforts to settle homeless offenders in accommodation as a first priority. For many of the cases studied here this seemed to be an impossible task. Often men did not settle. Despite the efforts made on their behalf many men continued to roam the country, commit further offences and appear again in court.

It would be incorrect, however, to see the failure of treatment as the result of inadequate assessment. All the officers concerned with the care of homeless men repeatedly pointed out that the lack of resources often prevented the giving of the necessary treatment. First, the accommodation available was inadequate because of insufficient variety, and this meant that some men were placed in situations which failed to meet their needs. Second, although officers devoted a good deal of time to those men with the greatest problems there was not sufficient time to resolve them. The officers' efforts had to be devoted mainly to short term difficulties, so long-term planning was not a feature of the treatment. Long-term planning was reserved almost exclusively for those in whom the problem of homelessness was slight and who were seen as being more hopeful cases.

It is possible that a large proportion of homeless offenders are, as the probation officers suggested, 'hopeless' cases, for whom treatment in the community is a complete waste of time and resources. It is equally possible that almost all homeless offenders could be treated adequately in the community if treatment were better matched to real needs. The research described in this report did not show which, if either, of these statements is correct.

APPENDIX I

Forms used in the Analysis of Social Enquiry Reports
and Probation Officers' Records

A. Social enquiry reports

The form shown below was used for the content analysis of the social enquiry reports collected for Sample 1. Items 6, 7, 8 and 9 were not used in the statistical analysis because the reports did not give the information required in a large proportion of the cases.

1. Name.   2. Date of Birth.   3. Age.

4. Marital Status: Single; Married/cohabiting; Separated/Divorced; Widowed.

5. Type of homelessness:

Vagrant	
At risk	
Transient	

Give brief description of homelessness.

6. Childhood: In care of local authority

In care of local authority	
Parents separated or divorced	
One parent family	
No information	

7. Family relationships:

Good	
Moderate	
Poor	

8. Employment record said to be: Good

Good	
Moderate	
Poor	

9. Unsatisfactory employment record for: Less than 1 year

Less than 1 year	
Between 1 and 3 years	
More than 3 years	
No information	
Not applicable	

43

10. Nature of probation officer's recommendation: For probation

Against probation

None

11. The sentence imposed.

B. Probation officers' records

Where offenders in Sample 1 were placed on probation they were followed up for a period of 12 months and a content analysis of the supervising officers' records was undertaken using the form below. Item 4 was not used in the statistical analysis because the records did not give the information required in a large proportion of the cases.

1. Name.

2. Homelessness
   Tick that which applies and give a brief description:
   (a) The client returns home and stays there.
   (b) The client settles in relatively stable accommodation.
   (c) The client remains homeless.
   (d) Other outcome.

3. Note briefly what action (if any) the supervising officer took to resolve homelessness.

4. Employment:
   (a) Number of jobs during the follow-up period.
   (b) The total time employed.
   (c) Note briefly any action taken by the supervising officer to find the client work.

APPENDIX II

The Homeless Offenders' Schedule and Content Analysis Form for Probation Officers' Records

A. The homeless offenders' schedule

Officers completed the schedule shown below for each of the homeless men they supervised. Items 11, 12 and 13 were excluded from the analysis because they were found to apply to only a few of the cases.

Homeless Offenders' Schedule

Client:
Officer:
Office:
Date:

This questionnaire should be completed for clients who have no settled address. Where details are not known in the first instance, they should be added retrospectively as soon as the supervising officer can provide the information.
The questionnaire should be returned to the research worker as soon as possible.

1. Date of birth.   2. Age.

3. Criminal history

Number of convictions recorded: One

Two/three

Four/five

Six/seven

Eight plus

Details of last two convictions:

Date	Offence (in brief)	Sentence (in brief)

45

4. Marital status: Single

                                 Married/Cohabiting

                                 Widowed

                                 Separated/Divorced

5. Work

     Is the client: employed

                             unemployed

6. Is there evidence that an unsteady work record has been a problem for the client in the past?

                                   very much so

                                   slightly

                                 not at all

7. Health

Is there any evidence that a psychiatric examination has been made on the client in the recent past?

                                 yes

                                 no

If yes, did the result show that mental illness is a problem for the client?

                                 very much so

                                 slightly

                                 not at all

Please give brief details:

If no, in your opinion is mental illness a problem for the client?

                                 very much so

                                 slightly

                                 not at all

Please give brief details:

8. Is physical ill-health or disability a problem for the client?

very much so ☐

slightly ☐

not at all ☐

Please give brief details:

9. Social contacts
   In his social life would you say that the client:

is a lone wolf ☐

mixes mainly with criminals ☐

mixes mainly with non-criminals ☐

don't know ☐

10. Accommodation
    Is the client at present in accommodation:

yes ☐

no ☐

If no, please pass on to question 15.

11. Is there any person in the place where the client lives who has a particularly close relation-ship with him?

yes ☐

no ☐

If yes, who?

12. Would you describe the affection of this person for the client as:

over-protective ☐

warm ☐

indifferent ☐

hostile/rejective ☐

don't know/not applicable ☐

47

13. Would you describe the emotional ties of the client to that person as being:

attached

indifferent

hostile

don't know

14. Are any of the people that the client is living with known to have criminal tendencies?

very much so

slightly

not at all

don't know

15. Assessment of homelessness
The past: to what extent has unstable accommodation been an established pattern of this man's background?

very much so

moderately

slightly

not at all

The present: into which of the following groups does the client's current accommodation fall?

sleeping rough

very unstable accommodation

fairly unstable accommodation

fairly stable accommodation

very stable accommodation

Prognosis: which of the following statements* comes nearest to your view of the client's future?

the client has a home to go to and is likely to return there

the client is likely to settle in relatively stable accommodation

the client is likely to remain of no fixed abode

* If none of the statements conforms to your view of the likely situation please give further details.

16. Assessment of deviance
    For each of the problems listed please tick the column which best describes its severity or absence:

	Very Severe	Severe	Moderate	Mild	Absent	Don't Know
Little conscience*						
Drunkenness						
Anti-authority attitudes						
Dishonesty						
Irresponsibility						
Callousness						
Delinquent tendencies						
Untruthfulness						
No loyalties						
Anti-social attitudes						

* e.g. If the client has no conscience about his criminal behaviour, the problem of 'Little conscience' would be assessed as very severe.

B. The content analysis form for probation officers' records

The form shown below was used for the content analysis of records for the 1969 and 1970 samples of homeless men (Samples 2 and 6) and for the analysis of records for Sample 3. Item 10 was excluded from the analysis because information was not available for a large number of cases.

Content Analysis of After-Care Record

1. Name.

2. Case number.

3. Number of previous convictions ☐   4. Age ☐

Marital status: Single ☐

Married/Cohabiting ☐

Separated/Divorced ☐

Widowed ☐

49

6. Recorded contacts with client: Office interviews

           Visits to client's residence

           Telephone

           Other (specify)

Total number of contacts

Total length of contact (maximum six months)..

7. First presenting problems: Money

           Clothes

           Accommodation

           Other material assistance

           Employment

           Other (specify)

           None

8. Action by probation officer at first interview:

           Gives cash

           Gives clothes/letter for clothes

           Assists in finding accommodation

           Gives other material assistance

           Assists in finding employment

           Advises about employment prospects

           *Assists with practical problems

           **Refers to other agencies

           None

           *Specify: **Specify:

9. Is the client convicted again within 12 months of first contact?

           Yes

           No

           No information

10. Where was the client at the time of the last entry in the record or at the end of six months from first contact:

Hostel

Lodgings

Flat/Bed-sitter

Prison or custody

Hospital

Thought to be sleeping rough

Moved to another town

Left accommodation but no evidence of where he went

No evidence at all

Other (specify)

APPENDIX III

Deviance Scores

A. The assessment of deviance

As part of the National Study of Probation, probation officers who helped to collect information about the offenders in the sample were asked to complete a problem checklist on each case. This checklist consisted of 61 personal and social problems on which each probationer was rated as very severe, severe, moderate, mild, absent or don't know. These ratings were made within three weeks of the offender being placed on probation.

One way in which the problem checklist was analysed aimed at providing a measure of deviance using the following procedure:

(i) Judgement by research staff. Eight research staff, working independently of each other, and without prior knowledge of ratings by probation officers or of the outcome of cases, assessed each of the 61 problems as being factors related to (a) dependence, (b) deviance, (c) both, or (d) neither. Ten personality problems were selected on which at least seven of the eight staff agreed that the problem related to deviance only. These were: irresponsibility; no loyalties; callousness; anti-authority; anti-social; dishonest; untruthful; little conscience; drunkenness; delinquent tendencies.

(ii) Weighted scores. All the probationers were given weighted scores for each of the ten problems so that very severe=4, severe=3, moderate=2, mild=1, absent/don't know=0. For each individual the weighted scores on the ten problems were added up to give an overall deviance score. This gave a maximum possible score of 40 for a probationer given ratings of very severe for all the problems and a minimum score of zero.

B. A comparison between the deviance scores of the sample of homeless after-care cases and those of a sample of probationers

Frequency distributions of the deviance scores were worked out for the sample of homeless men (Sample 2) and for a sample of 379 male probationers, the 'V' set described by Simon [10]. Twenty of the sample of homeless men were excluded because of inadequate information. The combined median was found and the median test applied to determine if the two groups differed in central tendencies. As Table 26 shows, the homeless men had significantly greater deviance scores.

Table 26

Deviance scores:

a comparison between the homeless after-care cases and a sample of probationers

Deviance Scores	Groups of Offenders		
	Homeless After-Care Cases	'V Set' Probationers	Total
Number of scores above the combined median	85 (86%)	154 (41%)	239
Number of scores below the combined median	14 (14%)	225 (59%)	239
	99 (100%)	379 (100%)	478

$\chi^2 = 62 \cdot 5$ df = 2   p < ·001

References

1. Residential provision for homeless discharged offenders. Report of the working party on the place of voluntary service in after-care. HMSO, 1966.
2. Turner, M. Safe lodging. Hutchinson, London, 1961.
3. The homeless offender in the south-west of England. South-west regional group consultative committee, 1969.
4. Walmsley, G. R. Steps from prison. South-east regional group consultative committee. 1972.
5. Silberman, M. and Chapman, B. C. After-care units in London, Liverpool and Manchester in *Explorations in after-care*, Home Office Research Studies No. 9, HMSO, 1971, p. 32.
6. Silberman and Chapman. *op. cit.*, p. 12.
7. Probation and after-care statistics, 1970, Home Office, 1972.
8. Simon, F. H. Prediction methods in criminology. Home Office Research Studies No. 7, p. 121, HMSO, 1971.
9. Silberman and Chapman. *op. cit.*, p. 29.
10. Simon, F. H. *op. cit.*, p. 122.

II. CASEWORK WITH SHORT-TERM PRISONERS

by
Julie Holborn

ACKNOWLEDGEMENTS

I am indebted to Dr I A C Sinclair for his help and encouragement in this study: it was part of the 'Midlands Experiment in Social Work in Prisons' for which he had responsibility. I thank too Miss Margaret Shaw, whose report on another part of the experiment has been reported in No. 22 of these studies.

I valued the helpful assistance that prison and probation staff in Winson Green, Stafford and Drake Hall prisons gave me, despite the many other demands on their time.

JULIE HOLBORN

CHAPTER 1

Outline of the Study

Many changes have taken place within the penal system. One of these is the increasingly important role that casework plays in the rehabilitation of offenders. This study examined some aspects of the problem of doing casework with short-term prisoners, and in particular, the difficulties that their attitudes can present.

Research aims

The study had four broad aims:

1. To examine prisoners' perceptions and their problems. This included both the problems that worried them during their sentence, and also their perception of their criminal behaviour;

2. To examine the kind of help prisoners wanted from prison welfare officers in prison and from probation officers outside; also to find out whether or not the men were satisfied with the help they had received from prison welfare departments;

3. To examine the way in which the working of the prison welfare departments was affected by prisoners' attitudes;

4. To consider the implications the findings have for casework in prisons.

Sampling, data collection and analysis

The sample comprised men serving sentences of between one and nine months for criminal offences, all of whom would be eligible for voluntary after-care on discharge. Men serving less than one month were excluded from the sample because of the difficulties of organising interviews. Men imprisoned for civil offences, such as debt or non-payment of fine, were excluded for the same reason, and also because it was felt that civil prisoners fell into a category of their own.

The sample was taken from three prisons, which together provided a wide range of prisoners likely to be reasonably representative of short-term prisoners generally. The prisons were Winson Green (closed, local), Drake Hall (open, training) and Stafford (closed, training, for prisoners under 21 and other men in prison for the first time). The sample comprised 120 men; 40 were selected from each prison by taking random samples of expected discharges at monthly intervals during a three months period between September and December 1969.

Most of the data comes from the research worker's interviews with prisoners in the sample. She interviewed each prisoner, one or two weeks before his discharge, for approximately one and a half hours; prison officers were not present during these interviews. Officers who called the men up for interview were asked to explain its general purpose and give the men the option of declining to be interviewed. Despite the risk of distortion in such explanations*, the procedure was adopted both to avoid causing some men unnecessary worry by stopping them from going out to work without giving them any reason, and because it was felt that men who did not want to participate would find it easier to say so to a prison officer.

The interviewing schedule is in the Appendix 4. This was piloted during June–July 1969 on a sample of 60 men. Some of the pilot interviews were conducted at the beginning of the prison sentence, but these did not prove very satisfactory, mainly because men had not always had time to formulate their opinions clearly, particularly if they were in prison for the first time.

The research worker had no prior information about the men when she interviewed them: she later examined their criminal records and other sources of information. To each man she first explained the purpose of the interview by saying that he and some others were being asked to take part in a survey of prisoners' problems and their use of prison welfare departments. She emphasised that this was an independent survey and that she was not trying to act as an informer for the Prison Department or as an aid for the prison welfare officers. She then attempted to engage the man in conversation about prison conditions generally (the food, views about prison officers, etc.) before going on to use the interviewing schedule. It was hoped that this procedure would help to break the ice, particularly with men who had been extremely apprehensive about why they had been called up.

Interviews generally followed the schedule fairly closely. However, since the study was essentially an exploratory one, discussion was encouraged and some fascinating red-herrings were occasionally pursued as a result. The point at which a prisoner was asked to describe his past life varied from interview to interview, and it was usually when the prisoner provided the worker with a natural opening.

As the main purpose of the survey was to obtain a picture of prisoners' attitudes, it was not necessary to check the truth of their replies against outside information. However, one aim of the survey was to examine the working of the prison welfare departments and for that it was important to know whether accurate information was being obtained from the interviews; so, about half the schedules were checked against the prison welfare officers' records and the research worker discussed with these officers the nature of contact they had had with the prisoners concerned. On the whole, the prisoners' replies tallied with information obtained from the prison welfare officers, though there were three situations where discrepancies sometimes arose: some men who had been convicted of sexual offences withheld this information from the research worker; those who had had

---

* See P. Morris: Prisoners and their Families, PEP. 1965. She felt the risk of distortion was too great and no explanation was given to men who were called up for her interviews.

difficult marital problems during their sentence occasionally did the same; and those who were dissatisfied with the help they had received from a prison welfare officer sometimes omitted to mention action that he had undertaken on their behalf, or underestimated the number of contacts they had had with him. The research worker saw the criminal records of all the men in the sample.

The Chi-squared test of statistical significance was used throughout the statistical analysis and Yates' Correction applied where appropriate. Tables with numbers preceded by X are in the Appendices.

Plan of the report

Chapter 2 describes some of the problems prisoners had whilst living in the community: problems which would provide an opening for the caseworker. Chapter 3 examines prisoners' perceptions of their criminality, some of the reasons for it and their anxiety about it. Chapter 4 describes the problems men said they had while they were in prison; it also examines their perceptions of the prison welfare officers' role and their use of and satisfaction with prison welfare departments. Chapter 5 first describes the post-release problems that prisoners thought they would encounter, and their perception of and intention to use after-care. Then an examination is made of prisoner's replies about the relevance of casework to crime. Chapter 6 summarises and discusses the findings of the study.

CHAPTER 2

The Men in Society: Aspects of Social Functioning

This chapter describes the sample in terms of some of the problems the prisoners had while living in the community. Basic information about the sample is in Appendix 1. The sample was representative of the population of adult males imprisoned for indictable offences during 1969 both in terms of the proportion of men under 30 and in terms of the proportion of men having five or fewer previous convictions. Within the sample, however, there were differences between individual prisons: Stafford inmates were significantly younger than men in both Drake Hall and Winson Green; Winson Green inmates had been in prison more often than men in either Drake Hall or Stafford; and Drake Hall men had been in prison more often than men in Stafford (which catered for young prisoners and men with no previous experience of imprisonment).

Marital status

During the interview each man was asked about his marital status: Table 1 summarises the information obtained.

Table 1

Marital status when the offence was committed

Marital Status	Number of Men			Total	%
	Stafford	Drake Hall	Winson Green		
Married/cohabiting	19	24	16	59	49
Unattached (Single, separated, divorced etc)	21	16	24	61	51
Total	40	40	40	120	100

Differences between prisons were not significant, though there was a tendency for the Winson Green group to contain a higher proportion of unattached men than did the other two groups.

Heavy drinking

During the interview each man was questioned about his drinking. This was a sensitive area for some of them and the research worker usually waited for the prisoner to provide an opening. This procedure enabled some men to talk more easily about the matter when it was a problem for them, though sometimes the worker was out-manœuvered, as, for example, by the man who said . . . 'I knew you were going to ask me that! that's the sort of thing my probation officer used to come out with!'

On the basis of information obtained, the research worker attempted to assess whether or not a man could be categorised as a heavy drinker. Nearly all the sample were social drinkers and the point at which social drinking gave way to occasional bouts of relief drinking was hard to identify. Assessment largely depended on whether the man himself considered that he was a heavy drinker: it seemed reasonable to assume that if he did so, he probably drank more than his friends.

Other criteria used in assessment were the presence of one or more of the following:

(a) in or out-patient treatment for alcoholism within the last 5 years which had not resulted in amelioration of the problem;

(b) two or more convictions for drunkenness within the last year;[1]

(c) disruption of family relations through heavy drinking;

(d) disruption of employment through heavy drinking.

Using these criteria, 45% of the sample were classified as heavy drinkers, as is shown in Table 2. The category contained a great variety of drinking patterns; it also included a wide range of dependence upon alcohol.

Table 2

Incidence of heavy drinking

Heavy Drinking	Number of Men			Total	%
	Stafford	Drake Hall	Winson Green		
Present	16	15	23	54	45
Absent	24	25	17	66	55
Total	40	40	40	120	100

Since it is commonly assumed that heavy drinking is associated with personal or social problems it was expected that the heavy drinkers would be mainly amongst the older, more inadequate offenders. However, the χ^2 test failed to support this expectation: there was indeed a group of older offenders with a drinking problem but there was also a group of younger, more aggressive, heavy drinkers.

Other aspects of social functioning

The concept of social functioning used in this report has been adapted from that produced by Eugene Heimler.[2] An attempt was made to measure the four aspects of social functioning which were prominent in prisoners' accounts in the pilot study. Scales were constructed to assess the level of the individual's involvement in family relationships, work and social relationships; his geographical stability was assessed in the same way. A man could score from 1 to 4 points on each scale—a low score representing marginal involvement or instability in the area concerned, and a score of 4 points denoting a reasonable degree of commitment and stability. A more detailed description of the scales is in Appendix 2.

One interesting finding was that the various aspects of social functioning were inter-related. This finding provides hard evidence for something that most case-workers intuitively believe to be true. It also provides hope for their methods, since it means that help given in one area of a person's life has a good chance of 'spilling over' and affecting his functioning in other areas. Table 3 shows that those with tenuous family ties were more likely to have poor work records and to be peripatetic; similarly, reasonably stable family ties went with a higher degree of commitment to work and geographical stability.

Table 3

Significance of the association between four aspects of social functioning

Aspects of Social Functioning	Involvement with Family	Involvement in Employment	Social Involvement (Friends)	Geographical Stability
Involvement with family	—	$p < \cdot 001$	Not significant	$p < \cdot 001$
Involvement in employment		—	$p < \cdot 05$	$p < \cdot 05$
Social involvement (friends)			—	$p < \cdot 05$
Geographical stability				—

Scores on individual scales were also combined to form an overall social func-tioning score ranging from 4 to 16 points (see Appendix 2). Those with scores of 10 points or less were designated 'low scores'. There were significant differences between prisons: Winson Green contained a higher proportion of low scorers than either Drake Hall or Stafford.

Low scorers were distinguishable from high scorers in several ways: they were more likely to be aged 30 years or over (Table X13), more likely to have had two or more previous imprisonments (Table X14); their most common offence was more likely to involve property than motoring or violence (Table X15). In other words, low scorers tended to comprise the older recidivist. The following examples illustrate what the social functioning scores represent. 22% of the sample had scores of between 4 and 8 points. These tended to be men with no family ties, to have few friends or acquaintances, to work erratically (if at all), to move around the country continually.

3.20 was a typical example of men in this category. He was in his fifties and said he had started to drink heavily while in the army. After his discharge he was unable to settle down and his marriage broke up. He subsequently lost all contact with his family and friends. He said . . . 'I just keep on the move all the time . . . I can't be left alone to my own thoughts . . . I take a job, then, I just gets the notion I'd like to move, so I puts down my tools, washes my hands, collects my cards, and wow! I'm off on the next train.'

Some of the very low scorers were younger, but manifested the same level of disorganisation and broken ties:

3.04 was in his twenties and a native of Scotland. He had been in trouble as a teenager and had then started to drink heavily. After leaving home he came to England and travelled around its major towns and cities, at intervals visiting his parents. His life appeared to consist of train journeys and picking up casual acquaintances wherever he happened to be. He worked spasmodically when he needed money but had long since abandoned the trade to which he had been apprenticed. He said he had suffered from depression after leaving home and sought relief from this in drink. He felt unable to stop his wandering existence and ruled out marriage as a solution to his difficulties because . . . 'You can't get married when you wake up some mornings and feel right down, as if everything was against you.'

25% of the sample scored between 9 and 10 points. These differed from the previous group in that there were one or two areas in which they managed to function a little better:

1.09 was afforded some measure of stability by the proximity of relatives to whom he appeared to be reasonably attached. However, he lived on his own and said he had 'moved around quite a lot . . . I get itchy feet and have to move.' His movements were mainly confined to the area where he had spent his childhood. His lack of involvement in peer groups and poor record of employment pulled his total score down to 10 points.

53% of the sample had scores of between 11 and 16 points. These men had achieved a measure of involvement in at least two aspects of social functioning, though this did not prevent their lives from being remarkably unstable and unpredictable affairs:

2.08 came from a broken home and had had repeated convictions for motoring offences since the age of 14. He described his marriage as 'chaotic' and gave the impression that his behaviour was fairly promiscuous. He was well integrated into the local delinquent sub-culture and was reasonably settled from a geographical point of view. His employment record was erratic and he tended to regard work as a last resort. Consequently his standard of living fluctuated: if he was not on the dole he was spending the proceeds of a successful 'job' in night clubs or on expensive holidays. His record expenditure, he said, was £2,000 in one month (though this may well have been an exaggeration designed to impress the research worker).

Case studies are indicated by means of a reference number. The prefix 1 refers to Stafford Prison, 2 to Drake Hall and 3 to Winson Green. Thus, 3.20 refers to the twentieth man interviewed in Winson Green.

However, there were some men whose lives did not bear the almost universal stamp of chaos and instability:

2.12 seemed to be fairly proficient in all four aspects of social functioning. He had worked for some time as a heating engineer and then set up in business running a fish and chip shop. He also ran a scrap metal business as a side-line and it was this that got him into trouble. He was married, had 3 children, was settled in the area and appeared to have many friends in the locality. This gave him a total score of 16 points.

Such men, however, were the exception. The research worker's impression was that most of the sample were only marginally involved with, what might be called, the business of living and many were burdened with deep psychological and social problems. Nevertheless, some managed their affairs to their own, if to no one else's liking, and tended to take the view that it was pen-pushers (such as the research worker) who were society's real drop-outs. To assume that behaviour which contravenes the social norm is necessarily due to the problems within the deviant, exposes one to the sort of attack that traditional sociology has encountered from its phenomenological wing, namely, that normality for players in one game may represent the reverse to those who play according to a different set of rules.

Inadequacy

Because inadequates are the group of offenders whose crimes seem to be most obviously related to personal problems, it was decided to give each man an inadequacy score. This was used in the analysis of which prisoners in the sample used prison welfare departments and after-care. The score was compiled by awarding a point for the incidence of each of the following factors:

Age 30 years and over	1
Low social functioning (i.e. 10 points or less)	1
Heavy drinking (as defined for Table 2)	1
Theft the most common offence	1 (found by West[3] to be the typical offence of the inadequate)
Total possible score	4

Forty-five men (37%) had scores of 0 or 1 and were classified as reasonably adequate. Thirty-three men (28%) scored 2 points and were classed not very adequate. Forty-two men (35% of the sample) had scores of between 3 and 4 points and were classed as very inadequate:

3.8 described himself as an old lag. He had been brought up in an orphanage until he was 14 years old, when he left to become an electrician's mate. He drifted from one job to another and then joined the army. He was soon discharged because he was under age, but he later joined the R.A.F. He was eventually discharged after 6 years for the offence of receiving. For the past

40 years he had been in and out of trouble, mainly for petty theft. Most of the offences were committed when he was drunk . . . 'I wouldn't pick up a match stick in the gutter when I'm sober—I do it out of sheer necessity.'

In the course of his criminal career he had gained some insight into his condition . . . 'I've got a sense of insecurity—feel anxious all the time. My psychiatrist told me I've got an inadequate personality.' He felt that part of the trouble was that he couldn't settle in a job and part of the difficulty lay in the fact of frequent spells of imprisonment . . . 'You think of yourself as different, you become introverted and don't mix well.'

Summary and comments

Taken together, the findings of this chapter indicated that at least half the sample coped badly with the demands of normal life. Broken relationships, inability to settle in a job, 'itchy feet' and depression were recurring themes in many descriptions. It could fairly be said that these prisoners needed help and, moreover, that they presented the sorts of problems which are normally considered to fall within the scope of a casework approach.

NOTES TO CHAPTER 2

1. In his study: *Offences of drunkenness in the London area:* a pilot study, B.J.C., 2, 1962, p. 272–7, Dr. Parr took as his criterion of 'habitual' two or more convictions of drunkenness in a year. The Working Party for its report *Habitual Drunken Offenders*, HMSO, 1971 (para. 4.17) took three drunkenness convictions as its criterion, but appreciated that this was no less arbitary and was not necessarily more reliable than any other.
2. Heimler, E, *Mental Illness and Social Work*, Penguin, 1967.
3. West, D. J., *The Habitual Prisoner*, MacMillan, 1963.

CHAPTER 3

The Men in Society: Crime, Chance and Social Competence

This chapter describes what prisoners said about their offences, and the kinds of 'reasons' they gave. Part 1 is a straightforward description of their accounts of their lives and crimes, and Part 2 focusses on the importance they attached to chance factors in crime causation.

Part 1: Getting into trouble

Prisoners were asked by the research worker how they had come to commit the offences for which they were currently serving terms of imprisonment. If they did not mention associates or alcohol, they were questioned specifically about these possible factors when they had completed their description: this was done because these factors had regularly emerged in accounts obtained during pilot interviewing. At some stage during the interviews the research worker asked prisoners to describe the onset and development of their criminal careers: most of them provided natural openings for the topic to be explored. Prisoners' life histories were not standardised and the research worker attempted to enable them to tell their stories their own way.

Prisoners frequently related their offences to other aspects of their lives. Those aspects mentioned most often were (a) the existence of problems, (b) bad influence of friends, and (c) effect of alcohol. The following description groups the accounts around these three factors: the groups are not mutually exclusive.

Problems

Forty-two men (35% of the sample) mentioned some sort of problem when describing the events leading up to their offences.

Twenty-seven of them spoke of practical difficulties. Typically, these men said they committed the offences because they 'needed the money'. Thus, one man said:

> 'I had no money and no job. I was driving with a mate and we pulled into a garage. While the car was being filled my mate hopped out and robbed the till.'

Some had the worry of accumulated debts:

> One man had set up in business as a window cleaner, but said trade had been ruined by bad weather and he had got into financial difficulties . . . 'I had about £150 in debts. The gas was cut off and the rates and the electric were due. I was going round canvassing for work and I knocked on this door and no one was in. The temptation was too much . . .'

Quite often, practical difficulties were linked with other problems:

> 1.37 had been in trouble spasmodically since his teenage days. He said his wife suffered from her 'nerves' and had received in-patient treatment for her

66

condition several times. She was unable to manage on the money he gave her for housekeeping and had been in trouble herself for shoplifting and theft. All four children were eneuretic and their laundry bills were huge. He said he had 'done the meter' on previous occasions when they had been short of money. On the last occasion, he said . . . 'We had no money and I just took it out. The wife said I had to get some from somewhere and that was it.'

For this man, 'doing the meter' had become a customary response to difficult situations. There were other men who normally managed to stay out of trouble and only committed offences when they were under stress. These men had often been involved with delinquent groups in their younger days, but had managed to pull out when they married and settled down. However, when they were under stress, their old way of life provided a certain kind of security and familiarity to fall back on:

1.18 had grown up in a delinquent area and had been in a good deal of trouble as a teenager because, he said, he had . . . 'got in with the wrong crowd.' Despite family difficulties and marital rows over his drinking he had managed to stay out of trouble since his marriage. His current offence had been committed because . . . 'the wife was in hospital last year with a miscarriage and I got a bit behind with the rent and that. I had the opportunity of picking up a bit of extra money and took this stuff from the factory we were buying scrap from'.

Of those mentioning problems 18 (15% of the sample) described interpersonal problems among the events leading up to the committal of their current offence. Most of these were matrimonial troubles:

2.39 said he had only been in trouble since his marriage, which had been punctuated by rows and temporary separations. In describing his offence he said . . . 'I'd been drinking with a mate and he asked me if I would come along with him to get this stuff. So I went along and got it. The handler got copped trying to sell the stuff in a pub and gave away our names. I wasn't bothered what I did—I'd just been kicked out by the wife.'

Sometimes, marital stress precipitated offences which seemed to be designed to call attention to the offender's plight:

2.40 had been in and out of trouble most of life. When he was 10 he said his father had remarried and two girls were born . . . 'he gave them everything, he was always buying things for them and wouldn't give me anything and the only way I could get things was to steal. I used to pinch things from Woolworths and sell them to the children at school.' His marriage went fairly smoothly for 3 years but then he was sent to prison. His wife refused to have him back on his release . . . 'that was when I started drinking. I used to go round to see her because I couldn't keep away, but she used to be out until two in the morning. It got under my skin and I wanted to kill her.' On the last occasion he was convicted for stealing £1 . . . 'I was in this shop and saw the note on the counter—I suddenly took it . . . I couldn't stop looking for her and I knew if I did this I would be picked up and I wanted to be taken away from her.'

For that man, it was fairly obvious that marital difficulties were only one of many problems. There were several men like this:

3.7 was an elderly recidivist who described his trouble as being a combination of depression, drink and losing his wife. He came from a family where drink appeared to flow freely . . . 'I had arguments with the wife's family over the drink and that drove me into trouble. I've been in trouble all my life, mainly for totting* or receiving. I've always been drunk when I've committed the offence or else getting money for drink. I need a drink to sleep as I haven't slept well since I was blown up in the war . . . I also feel generally depressed nearly all the time.' In 1955 his wife died . . . 'I hit the hay then and have been what you might call an alcoholic ever since!' He had been convicted of stealing a boiler. He claimed it was all a mistake as he had been asked to collect a disused boiler from someone's garden and had accidentally gone to the wrong address. He was drunk at the time.

For one or two other men problems took the form of losing their wives or a near relative. They tended to be the most inadequate men in the sample, and the loss represented the removal of a supportive environment which had previously given shelter from the stresses and strains of life:

3.15, a man in his fifties, said he had only been in trouble once as a teenager. He married when he was 20 and the couple went to live with his mother. She had died 12 years ago, and he and his wife fell behind with the rent and were eventually evicted from their council house. His wife subsequently left him . . 'I only started getting in trouble after mother died . . . been in trouble ever since, I'm easily led . . . just do stupid things, like gas meters. I suffer with my nerves . . . sometimes I seem to lose my head and don't know what I'm doing—the probation officer has called me short-tempered.'

Only six men mentioned specific psychological disorders in their accounts:

1.34 suffered from agoraphobia and described himself as being unable to . . . 'stand people or stick a job—I just have to leave. I can't go into town without taking the back streets. I've shifted from lodgings to lodgings—can't keep friends. Sometimes I don't go outside for one or two weeks on end. Can see myself ending up on a park bench with a meths bottle.' He had been living on sickness benefit for two years and committed his current offence because . . . 'I didn't have any money.'

Others suffered from depression:

2.17 said he had started getting depressions while he was in the Navy; he had contracted V.D. at the same time. He left the Navy in 1946 and had been

---

* Offences involving scrap metal.

subject to periodic depressions ever since . . . 'I do the gas meters each time—feel fine when I've done it. I did the same one twice on one occasion and the second time it had nothing in it . . . Sometimes I get really bad: I've had to cover myself with a coat in the coal hole or I'd lie under the bed because I felt afraid.' There had been problems at home too, . . . 'the wife's personality altered when she was undergoing the change of life . . . she had a coronary in 1962 . . . I can't talk to her, she doesn't understand my depressions.' This man had just been imprisoned for breaking, yet again, into a gas meter. He described how the pressure had built up inside him until he felt compelled to 'do the meter'; his response was rewarded by a tremendous release of pent-up emotion and he went out and got drunk. A few days later he was picked up by the police as he wandered round the city in a stupor.

The above cases serve to illustrate how the prisoners' problems were seldom confined to one area of life, but were spread across their entire range of social functioning. Some were more likely to mention problems than others: these tended to be men who were over 30 (Table X16), men whose most common previous offence was theft (Table X17), and men who had a low social functioning score (Table X18). Many offences were impulsive, feeble affairs, involving relatively small amounts of money. Indeed there were instances where profit was far from being the prime motive and the offence seemed to be the offender's way of telling the world that he had reached the limits of his endurance. These offences bore a strong resemblance to those committed by the passive inadequates described by West[1] in that they represented the line of least resistance to someone overpowered by the pressures of living. The χ^2 test shows that inadequates were more likely to mention problems in connection with their criminal careers than were more competent men.

Table 4

Relationship between inadequacy and mentioning problems in describing criminal career

Inadequacy Score	Number of Men		Total
	Mentioned Problems	Did Not Mention Problems	
0, 1: reasonably adequate	6	38	44
2: not very adequate	9	24	33
3, 4: very inadequate	27	14	41
Total	42	76	118

No information available on 2 men

p < ·001   df = 2

Bad influence of friends

Sixty-five men (54% of the sample) said they had committed their offence with associates. The role played by these associates varied.

The general way of living of some men made it likely that they would commit offences sooner or later: they were 'at risk' because of their companions. Typically, the pubs or clubs they frequented provided the kind of atmosphere in which crime was made easy:

'I was out of work at the time and had no money. I was in this pub and heard some fellows talking about this stuff up the road and that was it . . .'

Sometimes the offence was conceived after leaving the pub:

'There were four of us, like, in this pub and we'd had a few drinks. We were walking down the road and saw this car with its window open . . .'

Offences involving violence had often been committed on pub or club premises:

1.35 had been in a good deal of trouble (shopbreaking, housebreaking, fighting) and seemed to be well integrated with the local criminal sub-culture. He described his current offence: 'I was in this club one night and this fellow came up and asked me where my tie was—you aren't allowed in without one. I ignored him but he came back again and asked the same thing. I swore at him and he laughed and went for me with a wine glass I hit him with a beer mug'.

Another group of men felt they had been drawn into committing offences by their associates and tended to minimise their own contribution:

2.25 lived in an area noted for its high delinquency rate, but said he had only been in trouble once before. He had set up in business as a taxi driver . . . 'I'd just taken the wife into hospital to have her baby and went round to the pub. A bloke there asked me to pick up some friends in Edgbaston so we went round. They loaded some suitcases into the taxi. The police drew up and that was it.' The suitcases, he said, contained some 50,000 cigars.

Sometimes men became involved with the 'wrong crowd' at their place of work:

2.37 said that he had never been in trouble before he started his last job, where . . . 'everyone was taking stuff. Don't know what made me do it— pinched cigarettes, whisky and so on. The stuff was all around us—so easy to pinch, it was just there in the wagons. Some people get caught and some don't.'

Sometimes men fell in with what their associates were doing because they were under some kind of personal stress, as in case 1.18 described above.

1.21 had managed to break from the gang he had associated with in his teens. He had left home to live with his girl friend but could not get on with the owner of the house and was forced to leave. Before the offence he had been living rough for three weeks and become very depressed. He fell in with his old gang one night . . . 'we went drinking and started talking: next thing we were screwing.'

70

Some men followed trades which led them to sail fairly close to the wind from time to time. The scrap metal industry was a typical example of this:

1.32 had had previous convictions as a result of pursuing this particular trade. On the last occasion . . . 'I bought some metal from a friend and paid for it. It turned out that it didn't belong to him—it had been on a private tip and he'd not realised this.'

Most of the men who had committed offences with associates fell into one of the above categories, though there were a few rather solitary individuals who had just 'happened' to have someone with them when they committed the offence.

The effect of alcohol

Fifty-nine men (49% of the sample) said they had been drinking before the offence took place, or they were drunk at the time, or they were stealing money to buy drink.

Many of those who said that they had had 'a few drinks' beforehand committed the kinds of offences already described. When a man was in the comforting environment of a familiar pub with a collection of bored and restless friends it did not need the influence of more than 'a few drinks' for a crime to be conceived. Others clearly had a drinking problem. The hard core of older, inadequate men were, perhaps, the most pitiful of all those interviewed:

2.19 had a long string of petty theft offences. His current offence was no different from those committed previously and he had been drunk at the time. He was in his late fifties and since 1932, had spent most of his life in prison. He had started drinking at the age of 12 . . . 'I used to have to bring in a quart for mother and she gave me half of it. I wouldn't be in trouble if it weren't for drink—I get drunk every night, it's the only thing you can do.' He lived with his three aging sisters and worked for three months every year; the remainder of the year was spent on the dole or in prison . . . 'it's better that way (i.e. in prison), you can avoid working in the winter.'

Some ascribed the onset of heavy drinking to a particular set of circumstances. This may simply have been a convenient rationale for their behaviour but, as likely as not, represented the point where they ceased to be able to cope with life's demands:

3.2 felt that his heavy drinking had resulted from a combination of circum-stances. He had not been in serious trouble until he reached the age of 40. Then his firm put all its employees on short time, he found that he was unable to manage financially, and he got his first prison sentence for breaking and entering. Disharmony at home, which had previously been smouldering, erupted when he came out of prison and his wife put an end to their sexual relationship. Although they continued to live together . . . 'there was nothing left . . . I couldn't accept that she didn't want me—drowned my sorrows in beer. Gets now so that I just don't care—just let go . . . I didn't care whether I came into prison or not—was quite glad in one way because it stopped me drinking.' His current offence had been committed on his way back from the races. 'I'd been drinking heavily and just went down and stole some cigarettes . . . I'd just had a row with the missus—she'd got a separation order out and I'd just let myself go . . .'

This group of older, inadequate offenders typically committed trivial and futile offences:

'I was blind drunk and picked up a brick and threw it through this car window. They did me for breaking into it and attempting to steal, but I didn't know what I was doing—how could I have been attempting to steal?'

Another said:

'I can't remember anything about it—I was found on enclosed premises. All I remember is sitting on the toilet and looking at a dog and it turned out to be a police dog!'

Several of those who were classified as heavy drinkers were under 30. Some of these were fairly boisterous souls whose social life revolved around a set of friends met in pubs or clubs. Periodic bouts of heavy drinking were the norm for all concerned, but those classed as heavy drinkers said that they consumed more than their friends and were becoming increasingly dependent on alcohol:

1.35 had numerous friends and acquaintances in his home area. Since his teens most of his spare time had been spent socialising with 'the wrong crowd' (as he called it). He had several previous convictions, including some for fighting which, inevitably, had taken place in the pubs he patronised. During the past year he had been unemployed and had started to drink more heavily. He said he went out drinking during the lunch hour and in the evenings—the latter sessions generally finished up in clubs and he was spending around £7·50 a night. (Although officially unemployed, he lived off the proceeds of various 'sidelines'.) He then began to drink on his own, rather than going out specifically to meet his friends—partly, he felt, out of boredom and partly because it had become a habit. He had been convicted of causing grievous bodily harm after being involved in a fight in a club.

Some of the younger drinkers were aware that the situation was getting out of control; they knew that they no longer went out to seek companionship and, indeed, felt that they did not really belong to the group they drank with:

2.21 was an unhappy man who had been unable to settle down after leaving the army. He vividly expressed the dilemma of one who knew what his way of life was doing to him yet felt there was no feasible alternative. After his discharge from the army . . . 'I found it difficult to settle down—was used to having accommodation provided and a certain way of life. I didn't get a job for a while—then broke into a shop. I don't like staying in one place—I've travelled all over the place, staying with brothers, mates or in lodging houses. I don't like conning the family into having me—they feel they can't turn me out, but I don't like lodging houses—they're dreary and you don't like spending the night in them. I go into the pub to get away from them. I like the atmosphere, music and so on. My brothers and mates all go—if I didn't go I wouldn't have any friends. I could drink orange juice, I suppose, but it's not much fun when they are all drunk and you are not—you're not talking the same language. They've not been in trouble, though, so it must be something about me—when I have the beer in me, I get a kick out of breaking and entering. I don't do it for the money so it's an expensive kick!' His current offence was for shopbreaking: he said he had been stranded in Walsall without enough money to get back to Birmingham. He was with a friend, who was also drunk, and they happened to pass a shop whose entrance was not properly secured. The operation was seen by several people in the street, and the pair were caught red-handed. While reflecting on his position he considered the possibility of an alternative way of life . . . 'marriage might be the answer, but it would be difficult as I can't be choosy after being in here (i.e. in prison) five times. I might be able to con her and then one of my mates would say to her "you don't want him." I'd have to go to a town where I wasn't known if I wanted to get married.' To do so would inevitably isolate him from his friends and the prospect of being alone in dismal lodging houses was more than he could face.

For a group of younger drinkers the situation had got completely out of control:

3.32 said he had started drinking at the age of 14 . . . 'I went with a mate and then found that all I wanted was the drink. I used to go to clubs and take away bottles of wine to drink in the park—used to wake up there next morning.' He said he had 57 previous convictions for drunkenness and was sometimes drunk for days on end. All his offences had been committed when he was drunk. . . 'I get depressed and that leads me to drink and that leads to trouble. The psychiatrist said it was because I didn't get on with people and was trying to get away from them because I was shy.' His current offence involved violence . . . 'I had just come down from Birmingham because my father was in hospital. They told me he had only a few weeks to live. I was very shocked—I'd been away from home for some time and hadn't written to them so I didn't know he was ill. I went out to see my brother and we went for a drink. A bloke in the pub picked on my brother and I just went berserk and smashed his face in.'

The offences of some of these younger heavy drinkers indicated the desperate straits they had reached:

1.23 was 28, though he looked 40. He said he had been in 'the usual sort of trouble' as a teenager. 'I started drinking when I was 15—everybody does it to show off. By the time I was on borstal after-care I was drinking quite heavily.' His family split up after his father's death and his brother had been killed in an accident three years later . . . 'after that I just went to pieces. I couldn't settle—travelled all over the place—couldn't stay anywhere longer than a week.' Severe depressions set in around this time and he went . . . 'on the booze morning, noon and night trying to lift them. I'm so restless, I can't sit still. The only place I can sit still is in the boozer.' He had been for treatment but had failed to see it through . . . 'all people say is "pack it up", but you can't just do it like that—people who haven't got the problem don't understand.' His offences had become increasingly trivial and obvious over the years. On the last occasion . . . 'I did the gas meter—I wanted some money for booze and that was the nearest thing.'

The non-conformists

Several men did not relate their offences to other aspects of their lives, but emphasised that they offended by deliberate choice. Some had been drinking and others committed the offence with friends, but these factors were not a prominent feature of their accounts. Twenty-nine men (24% of the sample) fell into this category. Their offences were no better planned or more efficiently carried out than those of men already described. Sometimes the offence was something a man 'just decided to do':

3.1 positively sizzled with excess energy. He stole cars because he 'liked speed'. Crime fascinated him . . . 'I get a real thrill out of it, especially going into people's bedrooms and taking stuff out while they are asleep.' (This was followed by a colourful description of one such escapade during which he had dropped a tape recorder while passing it through the window to an associate outside and had awakened the owner of the house) . . . 'every policeman knew me in Dublin—I can't seem to stay out of trouble.' His last offence took place because . . . 'I didn't feel like working one day—I had the Monday morning blues so I decided to go for a drive. We stole this car and went down to Stratford in it.' He then gave a detailed and enthusiastic account of the police chase that followed.

Several men showed a casual disregard for the forces of law and order:

1.7 was another lively Irishman who appeared to lead a chaotic life. When things became too hot for him in Ireland he came to England because . . . 'I heard that over here you don't always have people telling you what to do.' Since his arrival he had always managed to find a job with a 'fiddle'. . . 'I've never worked anywhere without fiddling—I'd rather get £10 a week on a fiddle than £20 with no fiddle. I've been in trouble for knocking stuff off at the places I've worked at—used to take everything I could lay my hands on and never had a guilty conscience about this, though I would have done about taking money. The sort of blokes I'm with don't think of it as a crime because everybody does it.' He went to great pains to explain his attitude to life . . . 'I'm always happy—never bother about anything—never let anything get me down. I've always been wild—it's not that I'm rebelling against authority, like you see in films: for me, authority just isn't there, nothing's there, I'm just myself and I go my own way.' His offence followed his usual pattern: he was a casual worker in a large firm . . . 'it was accepted practice that everybody took a bit of tot.* I couldn't take my bit out during the day so I came back later that night after I'd had a few pints. The security bloke caught me at it.'

Some had decided that a '9 to 5' existence was not for them and tended to treat the research worker as a well-meaning philanthropist who was somewhat out of touch with the existence of alternative life styles:

1.29 said that he had been brought up by both parents, until he was 13, when his father died. He started getting into trouble about six months later and was put on probation for stealing £1,000 worth of firearms. He attributed subsequent convictions to a sense of outrage, on the part of the police, at the scale of his operations. He claimed that, after being in approved school, he had never been caught for offences committed all over the country. His explanation of his way of life was that, when his father died, he had very little money . . . 'I want money and everything it will buy . . . don't like work, nobody does, it's a waste of eight hours a day. My father didn't have to work much (he had a shop) and we all had plenty of bread—suppose that's where I get my laziness from.' He felt that boredom at work was behind many of the offences that his fellow prisoners had committed . . . 'I need a change—can't stay in the same monotonous job for long.' The offence for which he was currently serving a sentence of imprisonment was no different from the others. He said he was in for . . . 'breaking and entering and a few little things like that. I needed the money—£28 a week is not enough—so why shouldn't I have it?' He planned his offences beforehand, unlike most of those interviewed. 'I'm not ashamed, I know it's wrong, but I regard this (i.e. prison) as a respite.'

Comments

Collectively, prisoners' accounts displayed several noticeable features. One of these was the impulsive nature of the offences for which many of them had been imprisoned. Typically, the offences were carelessly carried out and held little promise of substantial financial gain: these factors made it almost inevitable that the offender would be traced. Few men were professional criminals in the sense that they relied on crime to provide for their needs, though a number were involved in rather dubious transactions as regular 'sidelines'. Many men related their offences to other aspects of their lives; the exceptions were the 'non-conformists' described above. The aspects in question were generally current circumstances, in the shape of problems, bad friends or drink. The men seemed to feel that they had no control over their behaviour when in the grip of these circumstances and tended to regard their offences as inevitable responses to situations they found themselves in. General unhappiness ran as an undercurrent in many accounts and seemed to play a large part in lowering resistance

---

* Scrap metal.

to temptation: some men were depressed, some were drunk or bored, and others appeared to be carried along in the wake of their problems.

Part 2: 'Trouble just happens'

Since the casework approach to crime accepts the principle of psychic determinism, it was important to examine the extent to which prisoners themselves believed that there were 'reasons' for their offences, rather than assuming they were chance happenings. Such an enquiry was particularly relevant because many prisoners in the pilot study indicated that they perceived their offences as responses to adverse circumstances. The enquiry was a limited one, but produced some interesting material. One of the questions in the interviewing schedule read: 'Sometimes you hear people say that you can never be sure you'll stay out of trouble—it just happens. Do you agree with this or not, or couldn't you say?' The biggest single group in the sample, 67 men (56%) agreed with the statement, and felt that getting into trouble *was* something that just happened. Most of this group had a 'situational' perspective, that is, they felt that crime was precipitated by a particular set of circumstances. Some mentioned practical or interpersonal problems that might crop up:

'It all depends on the circumstances you're under: you might have a row with somebody and do something stupid.'

'I didn't go out to get into trouble—it was just the fact that the work slacked off and the money didn't come in as it should have done.'

'You can never be sure you won't be back: I might get home and find someone has been on at the kids and I'll be out of the door and on to him.'

One man who had been in trouble on numerous occasions saw fit to pronounce on the matter: 'Yes, it's perfectly true: I've no intentions of getting into trouble, but if I'm on the beer, or things don't go as expected, or my temper gets the upper hand . . .'

Others mentioned their associates or drink:

'It's how you are at the time—you might be having a drink with someone and he mentions a safe and the next thing you know is that you're in there doing it.'

'It can just happen—after a night with the lads you just go and do something for the crack.'

'It can happen quite easily: you could be out somewhere and someone starts performing (i.e. fighting) and that's it—you can't run away and leave your mates.'

'You can be sitting in a car with one of your mates and he's had some beer. He gets done for driving and you get done for aiding and abetting.'

Some men felt that the dice were loaded against them because they were known to the police:

'With my record I could be walking down the street and get mixed up in something I'm not the least bit interested in and the police would take me in.'
'Yes, this last time I was trying to keep myself straight and was caught with a razor in my pocket. I had no intentions—I was going to the public baths.'
'Sometimes your mates can be knocking things off and the police know you've been in trouble so they start accusing you. So you might as well be doing it yourself.'

Not all adopted a situational perspective; some felt that life was such a haphazard, chancy business that anything could happen:

'There's no positive answer to life—it's no good saying I'm going to lead a good life, you just don't know what will happen.'

'I agree: like this time—at 2 o'clock in the afternoon I had no more idea of coming into prison than I had of going to the moon. By 3.30 I was inside.'

Seventeen men (14% of the sample) found it difficult to either agree or disagree with the statement. Some felt that they had a degree of control in determining whether or not adverse situations arose, but that, once in the situation, all was lost:

'It depends on the kind of job you've got—if you've got one with no temptations you won't get into trouble. If you haven't got time on your hands you'll stay out of trouble, or you'll stay out if you keep away from the wrong company.'

'It depends—in one sense I don't agree because I can make up my mind I'm not going to get into trouble. But there again, if I get depressed and browned off and the temptation's there—that's it.'

'It's a matter of choice up to a certain point, but then, if things turn against you, you haven't any choice.'

Others recognised the part they themselves had played in creating adverse circumstances:

'I agree, but there again, you can live the sort of life to avoid a lot of trouble. My trouble wasn't hitting this lad with a glass, but being in the pub in the first place.'

Some felt unable to come to any conclusion about the matter:

'It depends on the crime—there's all sorts of different kinds of trouble.'

'It depends on the bloke—there should be a reason why they do it. Some people have been brought up wrong—you can't generalise, everyone's different.'

Twenty-eight men (23% of the sample) did not agree with the statement. Most of these stressed their capacity for choice in determining what they did:

'I don't agree with it at all—I don't intend to get into trouble again and I won't.'

'You've got to be daft to think that—you know what you're doing don't you?'

'It's entirely up to yourself: I kept out of trouble for eight months by convincing myself I wasn't going to come back.'

Sadly enough, those who tended to say 'it was up to yourself' were men whose lengthy records suggested that their opinion was wishful thinking. Some men emphasised fate, or destiny, rather than chance, seeming to feel that their lot was to act out the part that had been written for them. Eight men could not answer the question.

Comments

The research worker was particularly struck by how easy most prisoners felt it was to get into trouble. Indeed, it seemed to demand no more effort than getting caught in a shower of rain. Most felt that a trouble-free future depended largely on chance factors which were beyond their control. They seemed to feel that chance operated by producing situations which lowered their resistance to such an extent that it became inevitable that they would drift into trouble. Typically, they said that when these situations arose . . . 'that's it'. Some felt they had more control than others in preventing the occurrence of these situations, but shared the common lack of faith in their capacity for choice when actually overtaken by pressure of events. Their feeling that they drifted into trouble, rather than actively sought it, has some similarity to Matza's theory of neutralisation.[2]

It seemed that, although prisoners often related their offences to the circumstances they found themselves in at the time, they tended not to place these circumstances within the general context of their way of life. Chance, not poor steering, was felt to be the cause of accidents. General unhappiness seemed to play an important part in undermining their resistance to temptation. Many of their lives seemed to be precarious affairs, in the sense that adverse circumstances were almost bound to arise from time to time. Sometimes this was because of their particular problems. Sometimes it was because their social life brought them into contact with undesirable acquaintances and led them to patronise pubs and clubs where trouble was a fairly frequent occurrence. Either way, crime, for many men, seemed almost incidental to their way of life.

NOTES TO CHAPTER 3

1. West, D. J., *The Habitual Prisoner*, MacMillan, 1963.
2. Matza, D., *Delinquency and Drift*, Wiley, 1964. The interpretation of delinquency offered here is that offenders run into situations which neutralise 'the moral bind of conventional order' and leave them free to drift into delinquency. Drift in itself was not considered to provide the compulsion to thrust a person into crime—the thrust was considered to be provided by the person's own will.

CHAPTER 4

In Prison: 'Welfare—Your Link with the Outside'

Even if it does nothing else, imprisoning a man gives him time to think. Traditionally, prisoners were supposed to use this time to reflect upon the error of their ways. It is important to know whether prisoners worry about their lives, what they think are their major problems, and whether they perceive the prison officers' role to be rehabilitation, because these attitudes could provide the prison welfare worker with an opening for rehabilitative work.

This chapter is in three parts. The first covers prisoners' descriptions of their worries and their perceptions of the prison welfare officers' role. The second part describes the contact prisoners had with prison welfare departments, and the way in which their attitudes affected the nature of the prison welfare officers' work. The third part concerns prisoners' satisfaction with the service offered by prison welfare officers.

Part 1: Prisoners' problems

During the interview the research worker asked the prisoners whether they had had any problems on their minds during their sentence. Almost three-quarters of the sample had, and several men mentioned more than one worry. Only a minority of men had an anxiety-free experience of imprisonment.

Table 5

Number of problems prisoners mentioned

Number of Problems	Number of Men	%
0	32	27
1	38 ⎫	
2	26 ⎪	
3	16 ⎬	73
4	7 ⎪	
5 or more	1 ⎭	
Total	120	100

It was of interest to know whether some men were more likely to mention problems than others. Application of the χ^2 test showed that neither age, number of previous imprisonments, social functioning level, inadequacy nor heavy drinking made any difference to the likelihood of a man's mentioning problems. Marital status, however, did (Table X19): men who were married or cohabiting mentioned problems more often than those who were unattached. Perhaps the explanation for this is that the existence of family ties tended to be associated with greater involvement in other areas of life; thus, married men

79

had left more behind, and therefore had more to worry about when they came into prison.

Prisoners generally worried about the problems created by their separation from the outside world: none mentioned the social functioning problems associated with their offences. This does not necessarily mean that they were unconcerned about the latter, but it suggests that the difficulties arising from their current experience were uppermost in their minds. Since these were the things they defined as problems in answer to the research worker's question, it seems probable that questioning by prison welfare officers would elicit similar answers. Three categories of problem were mentioned: 'immediate' problems, i.e. those associated with their current separation from society; post-release problems; and, thirdly, a miscellaneous category comprising problems of prison life itself, personal problems and worries about the police.

Table 6

Nature of problems prisoners mentioned

Nature of Problems	Number of Men	Percentage of 88 Men Who Mentioned Problems
'Immediate' problems		
Practical	20	23
Family welfare	42	48
Interpersonal	31	35
Post-release problems		
Practical	27	31
Interpersonal	6	7
Psychological	4	5
Other categories		
Prison life	8	9
Personal	1	1
Police	3	3

Most prisoners were preoccupied with 'immediate' problems. Twenty had been worried about practical problems, such as hire-purchase commitments, electricity or gas bills, arrears of rent or under maintenance orders, lost property, business worries, and car insurance. The variety of practical problems was immense.

Forty-two men had had family welfare worries and 31 interpersonal problems. These tended to overlap. Some men had left behind unresolved family problems when they went to prison, and so existed in a constant state of uncertainty:

'I've been worried mainly about the wife and children: how they're managing. The wife was under pressure to leave me at one time, but now she says she's not going to.'

'The wife and children. According to her letters, she's not alright—she suffers from bad nerves and easily gets depressed.'

Because the possibility of direct communication was so limited, letters assumed a position of paramount importance and several men were anxiously waiting for news of their family affairs:

'The wife—I've written to her a few times to try and go back with her, but I've had no reply.'

Some found this kind of tension more than they could stand and reacted by passive resignation:

'I was worried about the kids—there are eight of them now and the bab got killed a few days ago . . . the wife wrote me a bad letter a few weeks ago and I was very upset at the time, but I've settled down now and accepted it.'

Others, however, continued to feel acutely frustrated by their inability to tackle their problems:

'The wife had an affair with someone. She wrote the next day to say she was sorry, but I got very upset. There's nothing you can do while you're inside—you can't really write, you feel so sick. When you see visitors you've only got half an hour—you just have time to say "hallo, how's the bab?" you never get down to discuss your problems. It creates a lot of mental anxiety.'

The majority of prisoners who mentioned post-release problems expected practical difficulties, such as getting a job, finding somewhere to live, not having enough money or any working clothes or tools. Some men linked these problems with general feelings of unease about the future:

'Wondering whether I can get back to work or not. While you're inside you get so reduced your mind just seems to be in a little box and you can only think along the lines of things in here.'

'What life is going to be like when I get out of here—are people going to resent me? Employers won't want to know—once people find out you lose your job.'

One elderly man, alone in the world and with a severe drinking problem, was extremely anxious about his prospects:

'What I'm going to do when I come out. I come out just before Christmas and have only got a few days to find a place to live. The problem is to get cracking quickly and I'm going to be in a mess, I think. Lodgings are very hard to get and they're not very classy nowadays either.'

On the whole, however, he was an exception: besides being mentioned less often, post-release problems also seemed to generate less anxiety than 'immediate' problems.

Only eight men found prison life itself a problem, most seemed to accept the conditions in much the same way as they had adapted to the services:

'I just don't like the environment—don't like this dirty, clutty place. You've got to put up with some right dossers here.'

In the light of most prisoners' preoccupation with 'immediate' problems, their perception of a prison welfare officer's role was interesting. All those interviewed had heard of 'the welfare' and one or two of the older residents commented upon the way in which prison welfare departments were now an accepted part of the prison regime . . . 'before there was all this welfare lark you just sat it out; now, everyone goes to them with their problems,' said one man. The men were asked what they thought 'the welfare's' job was, and their answers were coded according to the problems they felt prison welfare officers were mainly concerned with.

Table 7

Prisoners' perceptions of a prison welfare officer's job

Prisoner's Perceptions	Number of Men	%
Dealing with 'immediate' problems mainly	68	57
Dealing with post-release problems mainly	6	5
Dealing with problems of prison life mainly	0	0
'Help' unspecified	34	28
Don't know	12	10
Total	120	100

62% of the sample were able to be fairly specific about what they felt a prison welfare officer was there to do, nearly all mentioning 'immediate' problems. Basically, prison welfare officers were seen to be people who could do the things that prisoners felt least able to do for themselves, namely, grapple with difficulties outside prison. As one man put it . . . 'they're your arms and legs on the outside.' Since married men tended to have 'immediate' problems more often than the others, it was not surprising that many prisoners felt that prison welfare officers were largely employed to deal with domestic troubles:

'They're there for the welfare of prisoners—if your marriage splits up their job is to try and sort it out.'

'They sort out married men's problems—get you together again. They don't bother about girl friends.'

There was a tendency for prisoners to feel that a prison welfare officer's contribution was limited to ameliorating current anxiety:

'They mainly help with the wife and family at home. They can't do anything for you in here to make the time go easier and the time you need real help is when you come out. The only thing they can do is put your mind at ease—if you know your family is all right, you don't worry so much.'

Some felt that prison welfare officers assisted the custodial aims of the institution:

'People have all sorts of problems in prison which they take to the welfare. If they weren't there, a lot more would be jumping over the wall.'

The remaining 38% were unable to be so specific about their conception of a prison welfare officer's job. Twelve men said that they did not know what 'the welfare' did. The others said that 'the welfare' were there to help with any problem that came their way:

'They put your mind at ease.'

R.W.: 'How do they do this?'

'By trying to stop you worrying as much as they can. I would go to them about anything.'

'All I know is, they help you out. I don't know what for, exactly, it's all according to what you go for.'

To summarise: prisoners who mentioned worries had generally been concerned about problems relating to the fact of their imprisonment and consequent separation from their affairs outside. They did not mention the social functioning problems linked with their offences, which, if they existed, appeared to have been pushed into the background by their current experience. Prison welfare officers were perceived to be people who were employed to 'help' prisoners and were not, apparently, identified with the custodial staff responsible for the organisation of the institution. No one felt that prison welfare officers were there to deal with grievances about prison conditions. Those who were able to define these officers' role more closely described it in terms of helping with 'immediate' problems. Prison welfare officers were not perceived to have a rehabilitative role —their function was seen as linking inmates with the outside world.

Part 2: Contact with prison welfare departments

Prisoner coverage

Prisoners were asked how many contacts they had had with welfare departments during their current sentence. (Those in Drake Hall and Stafford were asked to exclude any contacts while in local prisons before transfer).

One sixth of the sample said that they had not had any contact with prison welfare staff. Three-quarters of the contactless men were in Winson Green: all but five of the 80 men in the two other prisons had had some contact with a prison welfare officer. Some of these contacts, however, comprised short, routine interviews and a slightly different picture is obtained when these are excluded from the analysis.

Table 8

Number of contacts with prison welfare departments

Number of Contacts	Number of Men			Total	%
	Stafford	Drake Hall	Winson Green		
0	2	3	16	21	18
1	16	8	9	33	27
2	8	7	6	21	18
3–4	7	11	4	22	18
5+	7	11	5	23	19
Total	40	40	40	120	100

Table 9

Number of contacts with prison welfare departments, *excluding* reception and discharge interviews

Number of Contacts	Number of Men			Total	%
	Stafford	Drake Hall	Winson Green		
0	12	7	17	36	30
1	12	9	8	29	24
2	4	6	6	16	13
3–4	6	7	5	18	15
5+	6	11	4	21	18
Total	40	40	40	120	100

The men who said they had had no more than a routine contact with prison welfare staff now comprised nearly one third of the sample. However, the number of men who had had five or more contacts remained approximately the same, indicating that about one sixth of the sample used the prison welfare service fairly intensively. If those who had contact (beyond normal routine interviews) are defined as 'users', the above table shows that there were significantly more 'users' in Drake Hall Prison than in Winson Green (p < ·05). There was no significant difference in the proportion of 'users' (as opposed to 'non-users') between Stafford and Drake Hall prisons.

It is of some importance to know what factors are associated with use of the prison welfare service. Application of the χ^2 test showed that neither age, nor number of previous imprisonments was associated with the number of contacts a man had with prison welfare staff. But marital status was: married men were more likely to be 'users' than men who were unattached.

Table 10

Relationship between marital status and use of prison welfare service

Number of Contacts	Number of Men		Total
	Married	Unattached	
0 (non-users)	9	27	36
1 or more (users)	50	34	84
Total	59	61	120

p<·001   df=1

The association between marital status and 'use' of the prison welfare service held good in each of the three prisons individually, but was most marked in Winson Green (Table X20).

An association was also found between 'use' and social functioning score: low scorers were less likely to be 'users' (Table X21), as were heavy drinkers (Table X22). This pattern was completed by the association found between inadequacy score and 'use' of the prison welfare service: inadequate men were less likely to be 'users' than were men more competent in managing their lives outside (Table X23). Table 11 assembles the information about inadequacy and use of the prison welfare services.

Table 11

Relationship between inadequacy and use of prison welfare service

Number of Contacts	Number of Men			Total
	Reasonably Adequate	Not Very Adequate	Very Inadequate	
0 (non-users)	8	10	18	36
1 or more (users)	37	23	24	84
Total	45	33	42	120

p<·05   df=2

Taking these findings together, it is clear that prison welfare officers in these three prisons managed to see most of the men in the sample at least once. However, when routine interviews were excluded from the analysis, it was evident that those who had the greatest difficulty in coping with life outside, and therefore stood in the greatest need of casework help, were least likely to be users of the prison welfare service. This accords with Shaw's finding.[1]

Problems and prison welfare departments

Another factor associated with 'use' of the prison welfare service was whether or not prisoners mentioned problems to the research worker: those who mentioned problems were more likely to be 'users', as shown in Table 12.

Table 12

Relationship between mentioning problems to the research worker and use of prison welfare service

Number of Contacts	Number of Men		Total
	Mentioned Problems	Did Not Mention Problems	
0 (non-users)	18	18	36
1 or more (users)	70	14	84
Total	88	32	120

p < ·001   df = 1

Because 'immediate' problems predominated amongst those mentioned to the research worker, it was apparent that 'use' of the prison welfare service closely followed prisoners' perceptions of a prison welfare officer's job. (They felt he was there to deal with problems arising out of the experience of imprisonment.) The reasons for 'non-use' by inadequates becomes clearer in the light of this finding: this group tended to seek prison as an escape from the demands of the outside world; they had left little behind that really mattered to them and therefore could not present the kinds of problems that prison welfare officers were popularly supposed to deal with. The overall association between mentioning problems and 'use' of the prison welfare service held good for each of the prisons individually, but was strongest in Winson Green and weakest in Drake Hall (Table X24).

Despite the association between mentioning problems to the research worker and 'use' of the prison welfare service, Table 12 also shows that 18 of the 88 who mentioned problems had not had any contact with a prison welfare officer. This finding could be a source of unease to prison welfare officers who have been troubled because some inmates with problems withhold from contact. On the whole, probation officers coming to work in the prison setting have been at pains to prevent inmates with problems from 'sitting it out'. When the research was undertaken, probation officers had been struggling for several years to obtain recognition for their role by inmates and staff alike, and the finding just mentioned could cast doubt on their success in achieving their aim. Accordingly, it was decided to examine the reasons why some men did not discuss their problems, in the hope that this would shed some light on the matter. All those prisoners who mentioned problems to the research worker were asked if they had discussed them with a prison welfare officer.

Table 13

Problems discussed with a prison welfare officer

Problems Discussed	Number of Men			Total	%
	Stafford	Drake Hall	Winson Green		
Discussed all problems mentioned	9	10	9	28	32
Discussed some problems mentioned	8	11	7	26	29
Did not discuss any problems mentioned	9	10	15	34	39
Total	26	31	31	88	100

Did not mention problems: 32

Table 13 shows that over a third of those who mentioned problems to the research worker had not discussed them with a prison welfare officer.

Application of the χ^2 test revealed that neither age, number of previous imprisonments, marital status, social functioning score, heavy drinking nor inadequacy score was associated with a prisoner's discussion or non-discussion of his problems. Prisoners also appeared to be unaffected by what they perceived as other inmates' opinions of prison welfare officers (see Table 17).

The one factor associated with discussion of problems was the kind of problem prisoners were worried about: those who mentioned 'immediate' problems (with

Table 14

Relationship between type of problem mentioned to research worker and whether discussed with a prison welfare officer

Discussion With Prison Welfare Officer	Number of Men		Total
	Mentioned Immediate Problems to Research Worker	Did Not Mention Immediate Problems to Research Worker	
Discussed all/some problems mentioned to research worker	48	4	52
Did not discuss any problems mentioned to research worker	21	11	32
Total	69	15	84

Did not mention any problems: 32
Mentioned only police/prison problems: 4

$p < \cdot 05$ \qquad df$=1$

G—28

or without other problems as well) were more likely to have discussed them with a prison welfare officer than were men who had not been worried about this kind of problem (but mentioned other worries, such as post-release difficulties).

This finding indicates that prisoners' perceptions of prison welfare officers' role did influence their decision to discuss their problems.

The reasons given by the 32 men who had not discussed any of their problems with a prison welfare officer were illuminating. Most (26) had not discussed their problem because they did not feel the need to do so. Sometimes, this was because they had obtained help from other quarters, such as an outside probation officer. Sometimes, the problems had blown over by the time a prisoner had got round to wondering if he should discuss them:

'I had a letter from the wife saying that she was going to leave me, so I put down to see the welfare. Next day, though, I got a letter saying everything was all right so I didn't bother to go.'

In other instances problems did not seem to cause a great deal of anxiety; this was particularly true of post-release problems:

'I shall need a job when I get out of here, but I'll see about it when I'm out.'

Some prisoners' anxiety was rather diffuse; this may have made it difficult for them to find a concrete presenting problem to take to the prison welfare officer:

'I can't help wondering how the wife's getting on . . .'

'I sometimes wonder what will happen when I come out of here . . .'

A few (8) gave other reasons. One or two felt that their problem fell outside the prison welfare officer's function. One man was worried about his future employment, but had not discussed it:

'They're not going to see if there's a vacancy for you—you've got to do it for yourself.'

Two men gave the prison welfare officer's lack of interest or inefficiency as reasons for not discussing their problems:

'I didn't consider going to see him—some blokes say they're very slow so I just kept my worries to myself.'

'They have so many to see.'

Others had not felt like talking, or disliked discussing personal affairs. Two men said they did not want what they perceived to be authority figures interfering in their lives.

Collectively, these findings showed that prison welfare officers had managed to establish themselves as 'helpers', though not perhaps with the problems they felt were most important. When prisoners were worried about 'immediate' problems and had no one else to turn to they went to the prison welfare officers for assistance. Unfortunately, those unable to present 'immediate' problems had little contact with prison welfare departments, and these included the most inadequate men.

Nature of contact with prison welfare departments

Those who had had any sort of contact with a prison welfare officer were asked to describe what took place, e.g. who initiated the contact, what kind of help the prisoner wanted, problems discussed, matters brought up by the officer, and action taken by him. The kind of help prisoners wanted was broken down into eight categories; part of this classification was based on Hollis's analysis of casework method.[2]

Table 15

Nature of help prisoners wanted from prison welfare officers and action undertaken on their behalf

Nature of Help Expected of Prison Welfare Officer	Incidence of Expectations		Incidence of Successful Action by PWO
To act as channel of communication with persons outside	31	'Doing' help related to problems outside	28
To negotiate with persons outside	40		32
To make practical arrangements for release	19		15
To link man with outside probation officer	2		2
To negotiate with prison authorities	19		15
To give advice/guidance	7		7
To allow prisoner opportunity for catharsis	2	'Talking' help	2
To engage prisoner in reflective discussion about way of life	1		1
Did not know what to expect/no help wanted	18		

The majority of requests were for prison welfare officers to take active steps to preserve prisoners' links with the outside world.

Thirty-one men had wanted the prison welfare officer to act as a two-way channel of communication with persons outside:

'I wanted my (ex) wife's address so I could write to the children. I asked the welfare and somebody went round to see her and the welfare told me the kids were all right. He wouldn't tell me what the address was though, and I was very annoyed about that and shouted at him.'

In their capacity as communicators, prison welfare officers were asked to relay all kinds of information:

'How the wife is getting on'

'Whether my money from the firm has come through yet'

'Whether the bab's out of hospital'

'Tell the family not to come up on Saturday as I'm being transferred'

'Tell the landlady not to give my clothes away'

Forty men had wanted prison welfare officers to negotiate with outside persons on their behalf; some had requested this kind of help on more than one occasion:

One man had been worried about his relationship with his girl friend as she had stopped writing to him. 'I hoped the welfare would talk things over with her and sort things out—she thought I was going to stay in here for ever. He got me a welfare visit and explained to her that I would be out as quick as I could.' On another occasion he went to the prison welfare officer about a van left on the road before the prisoner went to court . . . 'I hoped the welfare would get it moved on to a piece of ground, but he said "get your father to move it", but dad hasn't got a licence so the van's now gone to ruin.'

Others had wanted prison welfare officers to sort out rent arrears, negotiate with firms where they had run up hire-purchase debts, settle gas and electricity bills and so on.

Nineteen prisoners had wanted the prison welfare officer to assist in making practical arrangements for their discharge:

'I went to the welfare to ask them for a warrant (to return to Ireland). They said I'd get one anyway, but I won't. So they said they would look into it, but I haven't heard anything—they just forget things.'

One man was due to be released shortly before Christmas. 'I wanted some money to tide me over the holiday; the welfare said they'd help—they're going to see about a grant.' He had also 'wanted help with getting a job. They got in touch with the welfare people outside (i.e. probation officer) and I'm going to see them when I get out.' In addition, the man had 'asked him for some clothes, but I don't know what he's done about this.'

Two men had asked the prison welfare officer to put them in touch with an outside probation officer.

Nineteen men had requested a prison welfare officer's help in negotiating with the prison authorities. Requests in this category were mainly applications for special letters or special visits. Although these could be requested from prison officers on the wing, or the Governor, some men seemed to feel that their application stood a better chance of success if it had the prison welfare officer's backing. This should not be taken to imply that such applications were unjustified—the research worker only detected two men who had sought to manipulate the system by inventing problems.

-/7-

ITEM ON HOLD

Some male offenders'
problems.

364.373 GRE

Very few prisoners had wanted 'talking' as opposed to 'doing' help. Seven men had sought advice or guidance about a particular matter:

> 'I'd had some bills from the income tax people. I'd never dealt with them before so I hoped he'd tell me what to do—which he did and I sent the letter off.'

One or two others had wanted help in drafting letters to solicitors or employers. Only two men went to a prison welfare officer because they wanted to 'get things off their chest'; and only one because he was concerned about his way of life in general.

Thus, prisoners took the problems they were worried about to prison welfare officers, hoping that they, like the 'deus ex machina', would put everything to rights. Few went to a prison welfare officer without formulating a specific request in their minds beforehand. As Table 16 shows, prison welfare officers did what the men requested in the majority of cases; this meant that they functioned as a 'lifeline' for many men whose contact with the outside world had been severed by the prison walls.

Prisoners' accounts of their contact with prison welfare officers illustrate, in a different way, the effect their attitudes had on the nature of work done by prison welfare departments.

For example, the research worker was impressed by the tremendous range of things that prison welfare officers were expected to do. Prisoners seemed to take their problems along to the welfare office, hand them over, go away and wait for something to be done. Prison welfare officers' casework records showed that some requests generated a considerable amount of work, some of it trivial and some of it immensely time-consuming. Prisoners were usually unaware of this: they were only concerned with the end-product of all the activity. One man, for instance, had asked for assistance in re-housing his wife: the prison welfare officer's record showed that he had made numerous telephone calls and written several letters, but despite his efforts, he was unsuccessful; his client's opinion was . . . 'they don't do nothing for you.'

Another feature of prisoners' accounts was their brevity: prisoners described their contact with prison welfare officers solely in terms of the problems presented and the help, if any, received. Further questioning by the research worker failed to elicit more than this basic information. Few men, when specifically asked if they had talked about anything in addition to the particular problem, said that they had discussed other matters. There could, of course, have been many reasons for concentration on problems; for example, prisoners may have had bad memories, poor verbal ability, hostile feelings towards prison welfare officers; they may have feigned indifference to conceal anxiety, and so on. However, perusal of the prison welfare officers' records indicated that the discussions they had with prisoners did indeed stick closely to the latters' presenting problems, and

91

there were few instances of the more general question of a prisoner's criminal behaviour being explored.

It was also noticeable that contacts between prisoners and prison welfare officers were generally initiated by the former: prison welfare officers tended not to take the initiative unless a prisoner needed to be informed of some change in his circumstances or his assistance was required in negotiations that were being undertaken on his behalf. The research worker was left with the impression that prison welfare officers were almost completely caught up in responding to demands and crises.

Part 3: 'The welfare do a good job'

The 99 prisoners who had had contact with prison welfare departments were asked whether or not they were satisfied with the help they had received. Six could not say and 18 had not asked for help. The replies of the remaining 75 men were grouped into four categories: very satisfied, satisfied on the whole, not satisfied on the whole and very dissatisfied.

Table 16

Satisfaction with help received from prison welfare officers

Satisfaction	Number of Men*	%
Very satisfied	21	26
Satisfied on the whole	29	36
Not satisfied on the whole	9	11
Very dissatisfied	16	20
Don't know	6	7
Total	81	100
Contact, but no help requested: 18		
No contact: 21		

* Includes prisoners whose only contact had been reception or discharge interviews; see Table 8.

Fifty of the 75 prisoners who had requested help on some occasion said that they were very satisfied, or satisfied on the whole with what the prison welfare officers had done. Typical comments of such men were:

'Yes, he did a marvellous job.'

'Yes, he did all he could to help me.'

'Yes, he tried to help—it wasn't his fault that things didn't turn out.'

The 25 men who were not satisfied with the prison welfare officers' response tended to give one of two reasons for dissatisfaction. Fourteen men criticised prison welfare officers for being ineffective in their role as the link between prison and the outside world. Staff were accused of being 'slow', 'muddling', 'forgetful' and so on:

> 'I don't seem to get no satisfaction. They keep putting you off and saying come back in a couple of days. If they ring someone up and can't get a reply that day they should come and let you know and say that they'll tell you as soon as they hear.'

When many prisoners are frustrated by their impotence to deal with things themselves it is easy to understand why speed and reliability on the part of prison welfare officers were rated so highly. Some prisoners had been promised help with post-release problems and were anxiously waiting to be told what had been arranged; one or two feared that they had been forgotten:

> 'I didn't want to stay in a Salvation Army hostel when I got out, so I asked the welfare to get in touch with a Probation Officer and ask him to find me some lodgings. They said they would, but I've heard nothing.'

The remaining 11 men were dissatisfied because a prison welfare officer either could not or would not do what they wanted. Prison welfare officers' inability to wave the magic wand was usually attributed to their lack of power. Some accepted that there was . . . 'a limit to the number of things the welfare can do.' Others designated officers as well meaning but ineffective:

> 'I think they mean well, they're definitely necessary, but they should have power to *do* things—they just can't get past the Social Security.'

Those who were feeling less charitably inclined wondered what prison welfare officers were there to do, when they could not help with important problems:

> 'I can't think that they're any use at all: if you go down to them and say you want something, they say they'll do their best and that's it. I prefer action to speech. Some people have worries at home and just want someone to talk to; they're useful then, but not if you want something done.'

Some men had been puzzled and angry when a prison welfare officer had refused to respond in the way they hoped he would. Some attributed his refusal to lack of interest:

> 'After my father died, I went to the welfare to get a day's parole for the funeral, but he wasn't interested. So I went to the Governor, but he wouldn't give it either and in the end I got the parson to get it. He does more welfare than anyone else here.'

One man had made several requests, all of which had been refused. He had not received as many letters as he thought he should have, and 'asked the welfare to look into the mail. He said "see the Governor", but how can I when I've been done for smuggling letters?' On another occasion he wanted 'the welfare to write to the court about a fine I've got. He said "get a letter and write it yourself".' Later on he had requested a welfare visit,* but 'he wouldn't have it. Seems as though he doesn't seem to care.'

In the last two examples, prisoners were angry because prison welfare officers had refused to take their side in approaching the authorities—something which none of the prison welfare officers in the three prisons wished to do unnecessarily. There was also some indication that prisoners had run up against the casework principle that social workers should not do for their clients what the latter can do for themselves. But, on the whole, these sorts of clashes were rare. Moreover, there were none of the complaints about prison welfare officers 'prying', 'asking too many personal questions', 'being nosey', etc. which Shaw[1] found amongst prisoners in her sample who had had extended contact with prison welfare officers. The nearest any of the present sample got to making these kinds of criticisms was one man who said:

'They want to know all about you, but they won't *do* anything for you.'

From these findings it seems reasonable to conclude that any potential clash between prisoners' perceptions of the prison welfare officers' role and the latters' view of their task was generally avoided because officers complied with inmates' requests.

It could be important to know what factors make for satisfaction. No relationship was found between level of satisfaction and prisoners' age, number of previous imprisonments, marital status, social functioning score, heavy drinking and inadequacy score.

It was expected that any previous experience a prisoner had of being on probation would affect his attitude towards prison welfare officers. However, this did not appear to be so: prisoners' opinions of previous supervision and supervising probation officers were not related to their satisfaction with prison welfare officers' help. This may have been due to the fact that only 50 men in the sample admitted to knowing that prison welfare officers were seconded probation officers. It was not possible to check how many of the rest did in fact know, but some of those whom the research worker informed of the prison welfare officers' true colours were surprised and clearly found it difficult to reconcile their unfavourable experiences of probation officers outside with satisfactory interaction with the prison welfare officers. One man spent a few minutes digesting this piece of news:

'It makes you think—but I don't think it will make any difference, I'll still go and see him. But, if there were two doors one marked "welfare" and one marked "probation officer", I'd go in the one marked "welfare".'

R. W.: 'You would do that even if you knew they were both probation officers?'

Prisoner: 'Yes, sounds silly, doesn't it, but I would.'

---

* Special visit in the presence of a prison welfare officer; usually to deal with family problems.

Others were rather shocked:

'No, they're not, are they? It's a trap, that's what it is—a trap. They're no good then. That's the last I'll have to do with the welfare.'

But these reactions were exceptional; most prisoners did not feel there was any inconsistency between their generally negative attitudes towards outside probation officers and usually favourable feelings towards prison welfare officers.

The sample were asked what they thought other prisoners felt about prison welfare officers, as it was expected that the perceived opinion of other prisoners would be related to an individual's own level of satisfaction. However, no such relationship was found, so it appears that prisoners are not unduly influenced by popular opinion in some aspects of their dealings with prison welfare departments.

It was interesting that other prisoners were perceived to hold very much less favourable attitudes to prison welfare officers than did the individuals themselves. Shaw[1] also found this with her sample.

Table 17

Perceived opinion of other prisoners towards prison welfare officers and satisfaction with help

Perceived Opinion of Other Inmates Towards PWOs			Own Satisfaction With Help		
Opinion of Others	No. of Men	%	Own Satisfaction	No. of Men	%
Very favourable	6 ⎫	27	Very satisfied	21 ⎫	62
Favourable on the whole	26 ⎭		Satisfied on the whole	29 ⎭	
Unfavourable on the whole	33 ⎫	63	Not satisfied on the whole	9 ⎫	31
Very unfavourable	42 ⎭		Very dissatisfied	16 ⎭	
Don't know	13	10	Don't know	6	7
Total	120	100	Total	81	100
			No contact/no help requested: 39		

As Table 17 shows, only 27% of the sample thought that prison opinion was generally favourable towards prison welfare officers. Typical replies were:

'They think they're pretty good, although there's the odd one or two who complain about them.'

'According to what I've heard, they're good blokes.'

The remaining 63% who answered the question thought that other prisoners did not regard prison welfare officers very highly:

95

'From what I've heard, they're not very reliable.'

'75% don't like them and 25% do.'

'Nobody has got a good word to say for them.'

'They all seem to think it's a waste of time going to them—there never seems to be any action and if there is, it takes months.'

'Most of them think they're useless: they say they'll do things and don't until it's too late.'

10% of the sample said they did not know:

'I couldn't tell you, I don't discuss things like that with any of the cons.'

'I don't know—it's not the sort of question you ask people.'

The way prisoners explained the discrepancy between their own opinion and the perceived attitudes of others was interesting. Some appeared to have dissociated themselves from other inmates:

'They seem to think they're a waste of time, but I think that's the sort of general chat you get in here: follow my uncle conversation.'

'You've got a mixture of people in here—intelligent and stupid.'

Others, in a rather superior fashion, explained that many prisoners had unrealistic expectations of prison welfare officers:

'According to what I've heard, some of them don't think much of the welfare. These are the people who expect too much—they expect them to work miracles.'

'People want things straight away and don't realise that things take time.'

Another explanation proffered was that other prisoners had not learned how to get what they wanted from prison welfare officers:

'I've heard people saying that they're a right load of rubbish. They say "they haven't done this and haven't done that" and I say to them that they haven't told it to the welfare right—they ought to bring it out and tell them the sob story; when they put down to see them they've got all night to work out what they're going to say.'

'Some of them in here—the "nutters"—if they don't get what they want, their opinions aren't very high. It's probably because they don't know how to use the welfare and go out of sheer aggressiveness. No one listens to prisoners who have got that sort of attitude.'

As Shaw[1] points out, the discrepancy between the public and private image of the prison welfare officer corresponds with findings in other prison studies. These suggest that inmates tend to overestimate the amount of opposition towards staff in the prison. Cloward, in a study of a military prison, comments upon:

'The frequency with which men conceal their desires for restoration from others, producing a pattern of "pluralistic ignorance"—the men were unaware of the number of others who felt as they did.'[3]

Finally, prisoners' contact with prison welfare officers was examined to see whether it had any bearing on satisfaction. No relationship was found between prisoners' satisfaction and whether or not they mentioned problems to the research worker, whether they discussed their problems with a prison welfare officer, the nature of problems discussed with him or the number of contacts they had had with him. The only factor that had any bearing on their level of satisfaction was a prison welfare officer's response to their request for help: these responses divided prisoners into two groups.

Thirty-five men had had every request for help successfully dealt with by a prison welfare officer; 40 men had not received the help they wanted on one or more occasions. Sometimes this was because the prison welfare officer had not informed them of what he had done; sometimes he had tried unsuccessfully to comply with demands; and sometimes he had told a prisoner he was not in a position to help with the particular problem. Table 18 shows that prisoners' satisfaction with an officer's help was strongly associated with his response to their requests.

Table 18

Relationship between prisoners' satisfaction and prison welfare officers' response to requests for help

Level of Satisfaction	Successful Action by PWO on all Occasions	Unsuccessful Action by PWO on one or More Occasions	Total
Very satisfied/satisfied on the whole	31	19	50
Not satisfied on the whole/very dissatisfied	4	21	25
Total	35	40	75

Don't know/no help requested/no contact: 45

$p < \cdot 001$ $df = 1$

These findings in no way invalidate the theory that prisoners initially approach prison welfare officers with a variety of preconceptions about their role and abilities, some originating from their previous experience of probation officers or from the public image of prison welfare officers, and some associated with attitudes towards prison staff in general. But they do indicate that, in the last analysis, it is what a prison welfare officer actually *does* for prisoners that determines their personal view.

Summary and comments

For most of the men in the sample, problems associated with the fact of their imprisonment took precedence over the more general problem of how they were going to avoid crime in the future. Although they were encapsulated in a separate world, most prisoners found it vital to maintain contact with what was going on outside. Prison welfare officers were popularly believed to act as a man's link with the outside world and the pressure of demands for help with 'immediate' problems left them little time to introduce a rehabilitative content into their work. They stood or fell by their ability to meet prisoners' requests for help, and it was success in dealing with most requests that was mainly responsible for the level of satisfaction with the welfare service. This success served to reinforce the popular concept of the prison welfare officers' role and thus maintained the pressure upon them to remain within a 'welfare cycle'. Their problem is illustrated in the diagram opposite.

One bad effect of the 'welfare cycle' was that those prisoners who had been social isolates when free had little contact with prison welfare officers: these men were so uninvolved in the business of living that they lacked the presenting problems that they thought prison welfare officers were there to deal with. It has been suggested that inadequates may commit offences in order to escape from society's demands. The fact that prison welfare officers were so busy enabled such men to bury themselves in the institution and rest undisturbed.

In conclusion, one may observe that prisoners have time to think and a case-worker might be able to help them think constructively. But, in 1969 (when this study was made) all the time and energies of prison welfare officers were fully engaged in coping with the problems that imprisonment itself created.

NOTES TO CHAPTER 4

1. Shaw, M., *Social Work in Prison*. Home Office Research Studies No. 22, HMSO, 1974.
2. Hollis, F., *Casework. A Psychosocial Therapy*. Random House, N.Y., 1965.
3. R. Cloward, quoted in Stanton Wheeler, *Role Conflict in Correctional Communities*. The latter article in Cressey, D.R., (ed.) *The Prison: Studies in Institutional Organisation and Change*. Holt, Rinehart and Winston, N.Y., 1961.

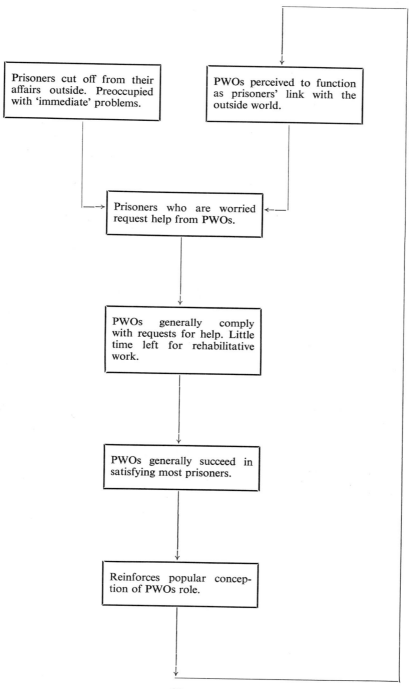

99

CHAPTER 5

In Prison: Thinking about the Future

This chapter is about the research worker's attempts to involve prisoners in thinking about post-release problems, and in considering the relevance of both prison welfare officers and outside probation officers to the task of rehabilitation.

The chapter is in three parts: prisoners' perceptions of post-release problems; the contact they intended to have with the probation and after-care service when free; and their perception of the relevance of prison welfare officers and probation officers to the problem of staying out of trouble.

Part 1: Post-release problems

The men were asked whether they thought they would have any problems when they came out of prison. Eighty-nine men (74% of the sample) mentioned one or more problems in response to this question, 26 men (22%) did not think they would have any problems at all and five men (4%) did not know.

An examination was undertaken to see whether some men were more likely to mention problems than were others. In the event, no relationship was found between expectations of problems and age, number of previous imprisonments, marital status, social functioning score, heavy drinking, or inadequacy score.

The kinds of problems mentioned were divided by the research worker into three groups—practical, interpersonal and psychological. Practical problems (such as difficulties in finding employment and accommodation, and lack of money) were mentioned by 71 men (80% of those expecting problems).

Interpersonal problems were mentioned by 22 men (25% of those expecting problems):

'Whether the wife will have me back';

'How the family will regard me';

'How I'm going to face my neighbours.'

Psychological problems were mentioned by only 16 men (18% of those expecting problems):

'Whether I'll be able to settle down—last time I couldn't and was all over the place';

'Getting depressed again—if that happens, I'll be back inside';

'It's the drink—I don't know if I can keep off it.'

No association was found between prisoners' expectation of practical problems, and their age, number of previous imprisonments, heavy drinking, or inadequacy scores. Interpersonal problems, not surprisingly, were more likely to be expected by married men (Table X25); and by those with high social functioning scores (Table X26). On the whole, the research worker felt that post-release problems created far less anxiety than 'immediate' problems. Sometimes this was because prisoners viewed the future through rose-tinted spectacles: ('once I get out of this place, everything will be all right'), or were unaccustomed to thinking ahead: ('I'll worry about the future when it happens'), or did not seriously contemplate changing their way of life and felt it would be comparatively easy to pick up the threads again.

Possibly the phrasing of the research worker's question focussed prisoners' attention on the difficulties entailed in moving out of one world into another. On the other hand, problems of bridging the gap might temporarily have eclipsed other, more general, worries about the future. Prisoners were therefore given the opportunity of expressing these more general worries; men were presented with 14 cards, each with a problem printed on it, and asked to sort out those cards carrying problems that they were worried about.* Four cards carried practical problems, two interpersonal difficulties, and eight psychological problems.

All but 16 of the sample picked out at least one card. The use of this technique altered the proportion of men mentioning the different kinds of problems; the

Table 19

Nature of post-release problems prisoners expected, using card selection technique

Problems	Number of Men	Percentage of Those Selecting One or More Cards
Practical Problems		
Getting work	51	
Finding somewhere to live	25	
Not having any clothes or tools	26	70
Paying off debts	27	
Interpersonal Problems		
How things will go between you and your wife	14	
How things will go between you and your family	20	30
Psychological Problems		
Having difficulty in settling down	30	
Being afraid you won't be able to cope with things	19	
Feeling that you're on your own	13	
Getting depressed	22	
Getting in with the wrong crowd	27	77
Keeping off the beer	23	
Stopping gambling	4	
Getting into trouble again	44	
No Card Selected	16	

* The research worker read out the problems to any man who could not read.

most noticeable change was the increase in the number admitting to psychological worries: 77% of the men who picked out at least one card selecting one or more cards carrying psychological problems, compared with the 18% who had mentioned psychological problems in response to direct questioning.

Not too much should be made of the percentages obtained for each of the three groups of problems expected, since the primacy of psychological problems may be due, in part, to the fact that only a third of the cards carried practical and interpersonal problems.

However, the fact that 44 men selected 'getting into trouble again', 30 men selected 'having difficulty in settling down', and that the problems of 'getting in with the wrong crowd' and 'keeping off the beer' were selected by 27 and 23 men respectively, indicate that, although practical problems loomed large in prisoners' minds, they were also worried about the more general problems associated with abandoning their criminal career.

The increase, from 89 men volunteering problems to 104 choosing cards on which problems were stated, was not surprising: people will admit to all sorts of things if the idea is implanted in their minds. But the fact that only 13 men had mentioned having three or more problems when interviewed, whereas over half the sample (62) selected three or more cards, probably indicated that they had problems in several areas of life and view the future with considerable unease.

Table 20

Number of post-release problems expected, using card selection technique

Number of Cards Selected	Number of Men	%
0	16	13
1	24	20
2	18	15
3	20	17
4	17	14
5	10	8
6–10	15	13
Total	120	100

An examination was undertaken to see if some categories of men were more likely than others to select cards. The sample was divided into two groups: 58 who, selected two or fewer cards and 62 who selected three or more. None of the factors, age, number of previous imprisonments, marital status or social functioning score, distinguished between the two groups. But, heavy drinking and inadequacy score did: three or more cards were more likely to be selected by heavy drinkers and inadequates.

Table 21

Relationship between post-release problems expected (card selection) and (a) heavy drinking and (b) inadequacy score

(a) Heavy Drinking	Number of Cards Selected		Total
	2 or fewer	3 or more	
Present	19	35	54
Absent	39	27	66
Total	58	62	120

$p < \cdot 02$ df=1

(b) Inadequacy Score	Number of Cards Selected		Total
	2 or fewer	3 or more	
0, 1 reasonably adequate	29	16	45
2 not very adequate	14	19	23
3, 4 very inadequate	15	27	42
Total	58	62	120

$p < \cdot 02$ df=2

These findings showed that those least able to cope with the pressure of normal life were most likely to be anxious about their future. As the inadequates were also the least likely to have had any contact with prison welfare officers (see Table 11), those for whom the future presented the biggest headache were the least likely to have had assistance in planning for it.

Part 2: Intended contact with the probation and after-care service

Information about after-care

Prisoners' perceptions of after-care will influence their use of the service. Men in the sample were therefore asked whether they knew that probation officers were trying to help discharged prisoners. One hundred and four men said they did. Not everyone, however, had connected after-care with probation officers; thus, their responses ranged from that of one man who had been in prison several times before:

'I know all about the "after-care", I always go down when I get out. I didn't know they were probation officers, though, that's a new one on me.'

to that of the man who was experiencing his first sentence of imprisonment:

'I'm going to see my old probation officer for help when I get out; I've never heard of after-care, though.'

Sixteen men (13% of the sample) did not know that there was an after-care service. This proportion roughly corresponds with McWilliams' and Davies' finding[1]: 20% of their sample of prisoners (whose sentences ranged from 14 days to 10 years) had not heard about after-care.

Although the majority of the sample were aware that they could go to the probation and after-care service for help when they came out of prison, they were rather vague when asked to describe what probation officers could do. Few were able to say more than:

'They're there to help discharged prisoners with their problems.'

Some were able to add:

'They can help you with a job'

'Last time I went they helped me with some tools'.

This vagueness stood in sharp contrast to the degree of clarity with which many prisoners had been able to define a prison welfare officer's role. This could have several causes. For example, prisoners may have talked about prison welfare officers more often than they talked about probation officers; so that an 'inmate line' had a greater likelihood of developing. Another reason could be that, while in prison, inmates share a common depriving situation and the prison welfare officer's role is defined in terms of this; outside, their situations vary so that it becomes more difficult to find a neat way of describing the role of after-care. Yet another explanation could be that prisoners' perceptions of the prison welfare officer's role was reinforced by the latter's compliance with requests for help; probation officers outside probably find it much more difficult to give these men satisfaction, partly because they are not so helpless outside as they were in prison, and partly because they ask for help with problems that probation officers have not the resources to meet.

Intended contact with a probation officer

Prisoners were asked whether they intended to see a probation officer for after-care help when they were released. It was assumed that the intention to use, or not use the service, would be a reasonably good predictor of post-release action since both McWilliams and Davies[1] and Burningham and Wood[2] found that prisoners who, during their sentence, decided to take up after-care did so in greater proportions than those who were undecided or who had decided not to use the service. Table 22 shows the prisoners' responses.

35% of the sample were expecting to have contact with a probation officer on their release. 20% of the sample were undecided about what they would do. 33% said they would not go to see a probation officer; but four of these said that, although they would not see the probation officer they knew, they might contemplate seeing another if they were put in contact with him. Most of the remaining 12% had not decided: some were unaware of the availability of help; others did

Table 22

Intended use of after-care by prisoners

Intentions	Number of Men	%
Definitely going	38	32
PO coming to see prisoner	4	3
Will see how things go/perhaps—if need arises	24	20
Definitely *not* going	36	30
Would not see PO he knows, but would see another	4	3
Had not thought about it	13	11
Does not apply—prisoner due for further sentence	1	1
Total	120	100

not seem to think the decision was important enough to have occupied their attention.

The reasons why a sizeable proportion of prisoners decided that after-care is not for them were examined. Neither age, number of previous imprisonments, marital status, social functioning score, heavy drinking nor inadequacy score differentiated intending users from non-users. Absence of any association between intended use and the three last mentioned factors, indicates that those who were potentially in the greatest need of casework help were no more likely than were the others to make contact with a probation officer. This conclusion is supported by the finding that no association existed between intended use and expectation of post-release problems: neither the number nor nature of problems expected (as shown by either method described earlier in this chapter), differentiated intending users from non-users. These results are quite unlike those obtained when this analysis was undertaken for prisoners' use of prison welfare officers (see Table 12).

Prisoners' experience of prison welfare departments did not affect their decision to opt for after-care; and intended use of after-care was not related to satisfaction with help given by prison welfare officers. Since an important part of a prison welfare officer's work is to plan for prisoners' release[3] it is disappointing that the goodwill such officers managed to build up amongst many inmates was not transferred to outside probation officers. Failure to transfer attitudes in the reverse direction (from probation officers outside to prison welfare officers) was noted in Chapter 4, so it seems probable that prison welfare and after-care are perceived to constitute distinct services, and probation officers in either setting are judged according to expectations of the role of the service in question. The fact that both services are manned by probation officers seemed to be of much less importance. Furthermore, the perceived opinion of other prisoners towards outside probation officers was not associated with intended use of after-care.

Prisoners' own opinions of probation officers they knew did not appear to influence their decision about after-care. However, the general attitude towards previous experience of supervision did differentiate intending users from non-users: those whose attitude was favourable were more likely to say they intended to use after-care than were prisoners with unfavourable attitudes.

Table 23

Relationship between intended use of after-care and attitude towards previous supervision by a probation officer

Intended Use of After-Care	Attitude to Previous Supervision		Total
	Antagonistic/ Negative on the Whole	Enthusiastic/ Positive on the Whole	
Definitely going/PO to contact	15	16	31
Will see how things go	10	6	16
Definitely *not* going	22	3	25
Total	47	25	72

No previous supervision/would see another PO/not thought about it: 48

$p < \cdot 01$ df $= 2$

Another factor that differentiated intending users from non-users was current contact with an outside probation officer: those who were in contact, or whose families were in contact, with an outside officer were more likely to say they intended to take up after-care than were those who had no such contact (Table 26). This is an important finding, and gives positive backing to the emphasis many probation officers have placed on the value of visiting prospective after-care clients in prison. It seems clear that after-care did not have an established role in relation to post-release problems and this was probably the reason why a prisoner's current contact with an outside probation officer emerged as a crucial factor in determining whether or not the prisoner intended to take advantage of the service.

Table 24

Relationship between intended use of after-care and current contact with an outside probation officer

Intended Use of After-Care	Current Contact with a PO		Total
	Personal Contact/ PO in Touch with Family	No Contact	
Definitely going/PO to contact	38	4	42
Will see how things go	17	7	24
Definitely *not* going	22	14	36
Total	77	25	102

Would see another PO/not thought about it: 18

$p < \cdot 01$ df $= 2$

The kinds of reasons given by those who had decided not to make immediate contact with outside probation officers, provide further illustration of the rather peripheral position after-care held in relation to post-release problems.

Table 22 showed that 24 men had not thought in terms of making immediate contact with a probation officer on release. Typical replies were:

'I'd thought I would go round and see him if anything went wrong, but I'm not thinking of going immediately. If I get into any trouble, he can help me out, can't he?'

'I hadn't thought of going, but if things get on top of me I'd go round—would always keep it in my mind.'

These examples suggest that after-care was seen as a sort of insurance by this group: its value lay in the fact that the individual had something to fall back on if the unexpected happened.

The reasons given by the 40 who said that they did not intend to make contact with an outside probation officer fell into three main groups.

Eighteen men had unfavourable attitudes towards probation officers. Some bore grudges against particular officers:

'After the bad word he put in for me at court, I prefer not to go.'

'He wouldn't be able to help me at all—he hasn't bothered to fix anything up although the wife has been several times about it. They've got hundreds of lads on their lists—why worry about the one who's still in gaol?'

'After the borstal after-care episode, he didn't want to know.'

On the basis of their past experience, several of the 18 men rejected the probation and after-care service completely:

'I can't stand their high-handed attitudes.'

'I wouldn't go because of the experience I've had of them.'

Some of the 18, however, were more discriminating in their judgement:

'There are good ones and bad ones, same as in anything else.'

'I can't talk to him and I want someone to talk to when I feel depressed. I'd go and see someone else, though.'

'I've no intention of going because of the things he's done. If they gave me someone else, it would be different altogether.'

It seems reasonable to assume that the 18 who rejected probation officers because they did not like them felt secure enough to manage without their aid (prison welfare officers were rarely, if ever, rejected on these grounds, probably because prisoners inside were not in a position to be so choosy).

Sixteen men said that they felt there was no need to see a probation officer:

'I've got no reason to go—don't need any help.'

'I can't see that they'd be any help to me—I've got a job and that's all that worries me.'

'When I'm outside I fend for myself—I ain't going to go around asking people to help me.'

'I can help myself.'

Six men felt they had problems, but did not think a probation officer would be able to help:

'I don't stay in one place long enough for them to do me any good.'

'They didn't do much for me last time—got me useless jobs.'

'I can't see what he can do for me: with a job, he tells the firm where you've been and it's a bit thick to have to work with people when you don't know how much they know. With the drink, it's a matter for the man himself: when I'm working, I don't drink—it's only when I get depressed.'

Apart from these six, however, the general impression gained by the research worker was that most prisoners had decided not to make contact with outside probation officers because they felt that they could manage reasonably well on their own.

Nature of help expected

The 42 men who said they expected to have contact with a probation officer when they came out of prison were asked how they hoped he would help. Table 25 shows their answers.

Table 25

Nature of help sought from outside probation officers

Nature of Help Sought	Number of Men
Practical help only	12
Other help, sometimes in addition to practical help	8
Not going to obtain help	13
Don't know	9
Total	42
No definite intention to see a probation officer:	78

Twelve men hoped the probation officer would help in practical ways:

'I'll see if he can get me a job—he could do better than I can because he's got more contacts.'

'All I want is a place, that's all.'

'He might be able to get me a travel warrant to see my son—he's there to be used, isn't he?'

'I want help regarding debts—he can help you arrange your budget.'

Eight men hoped for other kinds of help, sometimes in addition to practical help and sometimes instead of it:

'I hope he'll be able to fix me up with a job; sort out any family rows.'

'I've got no clothes. Also want treatment for depression—that's the biggest worry.'

'He might be able to help regarding drinking, because I do have a drop too much, especially at weekends. If I could visit him periodically it might help, as I can't talk to my wife about it.'

'I'll see him pretty regularly if I can and if I've got any problems I can discuss them with him. If you have a chat with someone like that now and again, it's a good influence.'

Thirteen men were not seeking help so much as renewing contact with an officer they knew:

'I'm going to thank him for what he's done. Anytime I want to talk to him I can just go along.'

'I'm not going for help, I'm going to apologise for conning him—he's been good to me.'

'I'm just going to see him—he's done plenty for me.'

Nine men did not know what they wanted from a probation officer:

'I don't know yet—it depends what I'm faced with when I get out.'

'I don't know really, he said he might be able to fix me up with some working clothes. He said come in for a chat whenever you're hard up and feel you may get into trouble.'

Thus, unlike the situation as regards prison welfare officers, many prisoners were not motivated by their problems to contact a probation officer, and they did not always have a clear idea of what they wanted from him. It appeared that the existence of contact with a probation officer was the motivating force and several felt it was worth looking him up, if only to ensure that he would be available in times of future need. It seems possible that the general vagueness surrounding after-care may, in part, have been due to the fact that prisoners did not know what situations they would face after release.

Part 3: Casework in relation to staying out of trouble

Probation officers inside and outside prison are employed to help in rehabilitating prisoners, but men in the sample did not see them in this light: they thought prison welfare officers were there to be their link with the outside world, and that outside probation officers had a rather peripheral role in relation to post-release problems. With a few exceptions, prisoners did not define a social worker's role in relation to the social functioning problems associated with their offences. Moreover, when prisoners described the sort of help they wanted, 'talking' methods, such as direct guidance, ventilation of problems, or reflective discussions, were seldom mentioned: prison welfare officers were generally sought out because of their ability to 'do' things that prisoners were unable to do for themselves, and most intended to use outside probation officers as a kind of insurance. It was impossible to know whether the focus on the practical and the immediate meant that prisoners were unreceptive of more insight-oriented casework geared to rehabilitative ends, or whether it simply meant that none had had enough breathing space to think about rehabilitation. It was therefore decided to ask prisoners some direct questions about their perception of the social workers' role in relation to rehabilitation.

The sample were given the statement:

Suppose we imagine that the welfare are interested in helping to prevent you from getting into trouble again. What is the best way that they could help so far as this is concerned, or don't you think there is anything they could do to help here, or couldn't you say?

They were also given the same statement, with 'probation officers' substituted for 'welfare' at a later stage in the interview.

Table 26

Whether prisoners thought prison welfare officers and outside probation officers could help them to stay out of trouble

Whether PWOs can Help	Number of Men	%	Whether Outside P.O.s can Help	Number of Men	%
Yes	35	29	Yes	46	38
No	77	64	No	66	55
Don't know	7	6	Don't know	5	4
No answer	1	1	No answer	3	3
Total	120	100	Total	120	100

Less than a third of the sample thought prison welfare officers could help them to stay out of trouble, and just over a third felt outside probation officers could. The majority of the sample in both cases thought that the social workers could not help with that problem.

The research worker divided the answers of prisoners who thought that social workers could help into four categories, derived from Hollis's classification of casework method. Table 27 shows the breakdown of their answers.

Table 27

How prisoners thought prison welfare officers and probation officers could help them to stay out of trouble

Casework Method	How PWOs Could Help: No. of Men	How Outside POs Could Help: No. of Men
Manipulation of the environment e.g. practical assistance	28	15
Direct guidance e.g. advice, sanctions	4	13
Ventilation e.g. providing a listening ear or general support	0	15
Reflective discussion e.g. about criminality	3	0
Other/vague	0	3
Total	35	46
Did not think caseworker could help	77	66
Don't know/no answer	8	8

The majority thought that practical assistance would be the best method of help from prison welfare officers. In the case of probation officers, however, 'talking' methods were mentioned more often.

Some men who judged practical assistance to be the best method felt that this would be the answer to all their problems. Many of these had a long string of offences behind them:

'If I had a £4 grant, a place to go to, a job, a set of working clothes, and if I could go out in the morning and come back in the evening and change into a spare suit and go out to the pictures, I'd have no need to come back inside.'

'Instead of going out of here with a £4 grant they should give every man a living wage for three weeks. I'll go out of here and I like a drink and some cigarettes and that's my £4 gone. So I borrow a bit and start out in debt; and, if I start work I've got to work a week in hand . . .'

One or two younger offenders joined the 'if' theme:

'If they could get me back home, if I had decent clothes to wear, had a job and got married, I'd live happily ever after.'

Some felt that the responsibility to stay out of trouble was their own, but thought that practical assistance would help to smooth their passage:

'He could see that I've got a job to come out to, but it's up to the individual to keep himself out of trouble.'

'They could try, but I think it's up to the person himself. They can tell you to do this and tell you to do that and you can take their advice. The best way they could help me is by helping me to get a job.'

Nine of the men who said that practical assistance was the best for prison welfare officers to help, thought that being put in contact with an outside probation officer would be useful:

'It would help if they put me in contact with someone outside who could stabilise me a bit.'

'If they got me a good probation officer it would help. If he visited me every so often it would stop me going out and doing things. The welfare could help with a job and that.'

Only four men thought that prison welfare officers could best help by providing direct guidance in some shape or form:

'The only way the welfare could help me is by trying to convince me that staying in one job, whether I like it or not, is better than walking in and out of work.'

However, 13 men selected this kind of method as being the best way outside probation officers could help them stay out of trouble. Some felt that the mere act of reporting would help to keep them in check. Others felt they needed someone to 'lay down the law':

'He could help me by telling me to leave the beer alone.'

'By telling me to keep my job, pay my lodging money and keep out of trouble.'

No one mentioned the method of ventilation to prison welfare officers, whereas it was mentioned by 15 men in relation to outside probation officers:

'The best way would be to have someone just to talk to. You could tell him what's been happening and he takes an interest.'

'If a man wants to keep out of trouble and has someone to talk to about his problems he will be O.K.'

Three men said that prison welfare officers could best help by enabling them to think about what they were doing with their lives:

'It would help to sit down and have a good talk to him—he would give me some advice as to where I went wrong in the first place.'

'They're people you can talk to and tell your troubles to. They could show you where you've gone wrong to get into a place like this. They've plenty of time for you—there's no rush.'

No one mentioned such help from outside probation officers.

On the whole, the research worker gained the impression that inmates felt that the social workers' rehabilitative role was rather limited. Prison welfare officers were perceived to be more limited than outside probation officers, possibly because many inmates held a situational perspective on their offences:

'They don't know what you're doing once you leave here.'

The reasons given by prisoners who said that social workers could not help them to say out of trouble were divided into four groups by the research worker.

Table 28

Why prisoners thought that prison welfare officers and probation officers could *not* help them to stay out of trouble

Reasons Given	Why PWOs Could Not Help: No. of Men	Why Outside POs Could Not Help: No. of Men
'It's up to yourself'	38	29
Irrelevance/lack of continuity between contact with casework and daily life	14	8
Lack of motivation	9	10
Does not need/want help	16	19
Total	77	66
Thought caseworker could help:	35	46
Don't know/no answer:	8	8

Table 28 shows that the distribution of reasons was roughly the same for both types of officer.

Nearly half the men in each case said the social worker could not help because only they, themselves, could do anything about this problem:

'It's up to the individual—willpower is the thing that counts. The welfare can't help you.'

'There's no way the welfare can achieve this at all because it's up to the man himself whether he gets into trouble again. The temptation is always there and you've got to take it or leave it.'

'I don't think so—they can only advise you, you've got to keep yourself out of trouble.'

Another group of reasons centred around the irrelevance of what happened in a social worker's office to the situations they faced in daily life. Some men seemed to feel that, to be helpful, a social worker would have to be at hand whenever they were confronted with adverse situations:

113

'I don't know—they can't help. Anything can go wrong—you can get stranded and land up in the wrong company.'

'There's nothing they can do—I don't go looking for trouble, it's only when my mind goes that it happens.'

'He couldn't help me unless he walked around with me and held my hand all day!'

One man made the interesting point that those who were near at hand were in a stronger position to control what they were doing than the more distant probation officer:

'He might be able to help, but the main person who can help is your wife—she can stop you going out for a start!'

Others felt there was no carryover from the social worker's office to their way of life because they, themselves, were unreceptive and the social worker's injunctions made little impact upon them:

'The welfare help me in here! I don't think they could—it's impossible. People can talk and talk to you, my probation officer used to talk to me for hours and I'd be going out screwing at the same time.'

'They can try to help you by talking to you, but it usually goes in one ear and out of the other. It's up to you really, if you want to be helped or not.'

Lack of carryover in these examples was not so much due to the social worker's inability to be everywhere all the time as to the fact that he was not someone who mattered to the offender concerned. Thus, one man described how he took more notice of people who were important to him:

'When I came out of Borstal, my brother said "you got a job?" I said, "no", so he said, "well, we'll see what we can do". He got me this job in a laundry and said "you're going to let me down". I said "no", and stuck it for four years just to show him. If they want to do any good, they've got to show they're willing to help. They've got to get behind you and drive you.'

A third group of reasons concerned the prisoner's own motivation to avoid trouble:

'There's nothing they could do to help—it's just the way you are, isn't it? If I got the chance of making a few hundred pounds, I'd take it.'

'I don't see how they could do it—if a person is offered an easy way of making money he takes it: everyone has got their price and will be tempted.'

'I'm a lost cause—I know I'm going to do it again.'

The last group of reasons were mixed. Some men felt they were beyond ordinary social work help:

'The only way they could help me would be to chain me to a fence so I couldn't get inside a car! It's just a fad (repeated offences for stealing cars) and no welfare officer can stop me.'

'I'm beyond welfare—a psychiatrist is what I need.'

Others were vague and gave no specific reasons for their answer:

'No, he can't do that, can he?'

'I don't think he can help with that.'

Some felt that they were not in need of any help.

It seems probable that prisoners assessed both the relevance of the social worker and the most appropriate casework method according to their perceptions and experience of what the social workers actually did. Their answers were thus influenced by their ignorance of the range of the social workers' expertise. In order to obtain a better idea of how receptive prisoners might be to casework, the sample was given sets of cards, each printed with a different casework method. They were asked to imagine that these represented the sorts of ways in which prison welfare officers (or probation officers) might help them to stay out of trouble. Then they were asked which, if any, of these methods they felt would be best for them.

Table 29

How prisoners thought prison welfare officers and probation officers could help them to stay out of trouble (using cards)

Casework Method	How PWOs Could Help: No. of Men	How Outside POs Could Help: No. of Men
'Getting things fixed up for you when you get out' (manipulation of the environment)	18 (29%)	26 (43%)
'Giving you advice and telling you what to do' (direct guidance)	4 (6%)	11 (18%)
'Letting you talk about your worries and get things off your chest' (ventilation)	3 (5%)	4 (6%)
'Helping you think about why you get into trouble and what you might do about it in the future' (reflective discussion)	37 (60%)	20 (33%)
Total	62	61
Did not select card: none would help	29	29
Unable to complete task	29	30

Nearly a quarter of the sample were unable to manage this task, usually because they could not read, but sometimes because it demanded too high a level of abstract thought; so these men had to be omitted from the analysis. An equal number thought none of the methods described would help.

Comparison with Table 26 shows that, when tested by the card method, markedly higher numbers than when they were questioned said that help could be expected of both services—prison welfare officers 62:35, outside probation officers 61:46. There was also a change in the kind of casework method considered most helpful. As compared with the previous emphasis on practical assistance from prison welfare officers (Table 27), most men selected the card carrying reflective discussion. Fewer men selected practical assistance as the best method, though this drop was probably caused, in part, by the omission from the analysis of those men who were unable to complete the exercise. However, it is likely that the shift of emphasis was due in part to the fact that using cards enlarged prisoners' conceptions of the help that was available. The fact that so many selected reflective discussion as the most helpful method indicates that they might be amenable to this type of approach by a prison welfare officer.

Comments such as 'I didn't know they could do this sort of thing', which were made by some men as they sorted the cards, support this explanation and suggest that these more receptive attitudes may have been masked by prisoners' mis-understanding of what social work in prisons was supposed to be about. Some of the men who selected reflective discussion also added the proviso that talking alone was not enough:

'Just talking doesn't do any good—you've got to know that something is being done as well.'

Cards selected for the best method that outside probation officers could use also showed a shift of emphasis, though in a slightly different direction. The propor-tion mentioning direct guidance or ventilation as methods decreased, while the proportion of men mentioning practical assistance and reflective discussion as methods increased. It did indeed look as though the supportive/insurance functions were originally chosen because prisoners were unaware of the existence of alternatives.

Summary and comments

In response to open-ended questioning, prisoners' replies indicated that post-release problems associated with the transitional period between leaving prison and regaining their place in society were uppermost in their minds. The research worker gained the impression that post-release problems created less anxiety than had the problems of being in prison. No association was found between prisoners' social characteristics and the expectation of problems. When presented with a wide range of possible post-release problems printed on cards, it became apparent that other more general difficulties associated with deviant behaviour were a source of worry to many prisoners. This was an important indication that prisoners might be receptive to a casework approach. Chapter 3 indicated that prisoners' perceptions of the causes of criminality differed in some ways from the casework perspective; and in Chapter 4 it was shown that prisoners were preoccupied with the specific problems of being in prison, rather than the more general ones of how they were to avoid reconviction in the future. How-ever, when given the opportunity, prisoners admitted to worrying about other problems, and this suggests that their perception of their post-release problems may not have been as divergent from the caseworker's view as it seemed to be at first: social functioning was a problem for many of them. Men who were heavy drinkers and inadequate were more likely to be worried about the future than the others.

Although most prisoners knew of the existence of after-care, their conception of its role was rather hazy. Lack of knowledge of a defined role appeared to affect both the reasons why prisoners intended to contact probation officers and the kind of help looked for. Approximately one third of the sample said they intended to use after-care. These were motivated not so much by need for help as by the desire to renew contact with a probation officer whom they already knew. These men sometimes wanted practical assistance but more often seemed to hope that the probation officer would provide general support on which they could fall back in times of crisis.

In response to open-ended questioning about the relevance of social workers to the problems of staying out of trouble, only one third of the sample initially thought that prison welfare officers or probation officers could be useful. It was generally felt that the former could best help by giving practical assistance and the latter by providing general support and guidance. It seemed fairly clear that prisoners' replies to this question were influenced by their perceptions of the officers' roles.

When presented with a range of casework functions printed on cards and asked to say which of these methods they felt would be the most helpful to them in staying out of trouble, different answers were obtained. Reflective discussion was most often chosen as the best way in which prison welfare officers could help, and this method as well as practical assistance were chosen most often as the best ways an outside probation officer could help. The cards seemed to have enlarged prisoners' conceptions of the help that might be available, and this suggested that a proportion of prisoners might be amenable to a casework approach that involved more 'talking' than 'doing'—though prisoners' comments showed that they felt that talking alone was not enough and practical action was still required.

NOTES TO CHAPTER 5

1. McWilliams, W. and Davies, M., *Communication about After-Care—an assessment of prisoners' knowledge of the after-care services*, British Journal of Social Work, Vol. 1, No. 4, Autumn 1971, pp. 381–407.
2. Burningham, R. and Wood, R., *After-Care or Through-Care?* Probation, July 1970.
3. *The Organisation of After-Care*. Report by the Advisory Council on the Treatment of Offenders, HMSO, 1963, para. 79.

CHAPTER 6

Summary and Discussion

The study had four broad aims. First, to examine short-term prisoners' perceptions of their problems. Secondly, to collect information about the kind of help
prisoners wanted from prison welfare officers in prison and from probation
officers outside; and to assess whether the prisoners were satisfied with the help
they received from prison welfare departments. Thirdly, to see how prisoners'
attitudes affected the working of prison welfare departments. Fourthly, to
consider the implications of these findings for casework in prisons. The sample
consisted of prisoners, serving between one and nine months for criminal
offences, who would not be subject to statutory supervision on release. It
comprised 120 men, drawn from the discharge lists of three prisons (Winson
Green, Drake Hall and Stafford) during a three months period between September and December 1969. The report is based on data collected by the research
worker from interviews with these men. Additional information was obtained
from casework records kept by prison welfare officers and the Criminal Record
Office.

Social competence and crime

Although the sample was limited to short-term prisoners, it was reasonably
representative, in terms of age distribution and criminal experience, of male
adults imprisoned in England and Wales for indictable offences during 1969.
59% of the sample were under age 30, and Stafford inmates were younger than
those in Drake Hall and Winson Green prisons. All the men save one had
previous convictions, and 40% had five or more. 43% of the sample had not
been in prison before—the majority of these were in Stafford prison. 31%
had three or more previous imprisonments. 62% of the sample had been on
probation at least once, and 36% had experienced statutory after-care.

Most of the sample were property offenders. 68% were currently serving
sentences for burglary or theft, 16% for motoring offences, and 13% for offences
against the person. A similar pattern emerged when previous convictions were
analysed: burglary and theft were the most common previous offences of 71%
of the sample.

The sample comprised a great range of both offenders and offences, and this
needs to be borne in mind when considering the general conclusions of the report.
At one end of the scale was the 20-year-old who had been convicted of driving
whilst disqualified and, at the other, was the old lag serving his twentieth
sentence of imprisonment for petty larceny.

Social information collected about the sample suggested that many men had
difficulty in coping with the demands of ordinary living. Thus, 51% of the sample
were unattached, either they had never married, or they were separated, divorced
or widowed; and 45% of the sample were classed as heavy drinkers.

Prisoners were given a social functioning score, obtained by summing their level of involvement in four separate areas of life. 47% of the sample were designated low scorers: their lives were characterised by broken or chaotic family ties, poor work records, tenuous social relationships and high geographical mobility.

They were also given an inadequacy score. 35% were classified 'very inadequate', typically being men who were over 30, heavy drinkers, whose most common offence involved property and whose social functioning score was low.

Taken together, these findings indicated that many of the men had ceased to travel with a society that went too fast and demanded too much. Crime, for them, seemed to arise out of a matrix of psychological, social and economic problems. They needed help and they presented the sorts of problems that, in other settings, might be dealt with by a casework approach.

One important finding was that the various aspects of social functioning were inter-related. Thus, men with loose family ties were more likely to have poor work records and to be peripatetic. This provides hard evidence of something that caseworkers have intuitively felt to be true. It also has implications for treatment since it means that help given in one area of someone's life has a good chance of 'spilling over' into other areas and thus influencing his total state of well-being. It suggests that there can be many different ways of tackling the same problem, since improvement in any area can 'spill over' and raise an individual's general level of social functioning.

An examination of prisoners' accounts of their crimes indicated that most offences were committed on the spur of the moment, were poorly executed and carried little hope of substantial financial gain. General carelessness made it almost inevitable that the offender would be traced. Few men were professional criminals. Very often, their offences represented impulsive responses to adverse circumstances. In these situations, prisoners' resistance to temptation seemed to be lowered by such things as general unhappiness, depression, drink or boredom. Others appeared to be carried along in the wake of their problems. To the outsider, many prisoners' lives were precarious affairs in the sense that crime was almost incidental to the pattern of their existence.

Prison welfare officers and problems in prison

The ability of prison welfare officers to do rehabilitative work depends in some measure on prisoners' perceptions of their problems and of the role of prison welfare officers in relation to these. Few men escaped with an anxiety-free experience of imprisonment: nearly three quarters of the sample told the research worker that they had been worried about at least one problem during their sentence. Married men were more likely to mention problems than those who were unattached. Those who mentioned worries had generally been preoccupied with immediate problems, that is, difficulties created by their separation from society. They did not mention social functioning problems associated with their offences.

All the men interviewed had heard of 'the welfare'. Many had a clear idea of what they felt prison welfare officers were there to do. They did not identify prison welfare officers with the discipline staff but saw them, essentially, as people who 'helped'. The prison welfare officers' role was defined in terms of the prisoners' most pressing need, namely, to maintain contact with the outside world. These officers were not perceived to be agents of rehabilitation: as one man put it, they were there to be a prisoner's 'arms and legs on the outside.'

Most of the prisoners had had some contact with prison welfare departments, even if only a routine interview, and approximately one sixth of them had used the prison welfare service fairly intensively.

It was clear that use of the prison welfare service closely followed prisoners' perceptions of the prison welfare officers' role. Users were more often married than unattached; they were more often men who mentioned problems to the research worker than men who said they had had no worries. Non-users were more often men with a low social functioning score, heavy drinkers and very inadequate men.

Prison welfare officers had succeeded in establishing themselves as helpers with immediate problems: almost all the prisoners who were worried about such concrete problems went for help. If matters were not discussed with a prison welfare officer it was usually because someone else was available to help. But, there was some evidence that more diffuse worries were not discussed, presumably because prisoners felt they needed a specific presenting problem to justify making an application to see 'the welfare'. Judging from prisoners' accounts of their contact with a prison welfare officer, most men went for help in the hope that he would solve everything. Few went without formulating a specific request. On the whole, prison welfare officers did what prisoners wanted and so fulfilled the role of intermediary with the outside world.

The popular definition of their role meant that prison welfare officers were presented with a tremendous variety of things to do. Prisoners seemed to be rather uninvolved in the solution of their problems—they handed them over and awaited action. It appeared that communication between prison welfare officer and prisoner stuck closely to the latter's presenting problems, and seldom ventured into the more general area of criminality. It was also noticeable that contacts took place on prisoner's, rather than prison welfare officer's, initiative. Indeed, the impression gained by the research worker was that these officers were caught up and carried along in responding to demand, and so had little time or energy left to introduce a rehabilitative content into their work. There seems to be no good reason for dismissing prisoners' demands as attempts to exploit treatment staff: prison does create very real difficulties for its inmates.

The majority of prisoners were reasonably satisfied with the help they had received from prison welfare departments: prison welfare officers were judged by their ability to respond to demands for help. Although, in the first instance, prisoners may have approached the department with a variety of preconceptions, in the last analysis, it was what the prison welfare officer did that really mattered. Dissatisfied prisoners criticised staff for an inadequate performance of their welfare role; thus, they were accused of being slow, muddling, forgetful, and so on. There was no evidence that contact between prisoners and prison welfare officers foundered on differing approaches to problem solving (as has been reported by Mayer and Timms for a sample of Family Welfare Association clients[1]). This was probably because prison welfare officers were seldom able to move out of a welfare role and therefore complied with prisoners' welfare-oriented expectations. Prison welfare officers' success in meeting requests for help confirmed them in their welfare role and drew them into a 'welfare cycle'. Since no one else in the prison could deal with prisoners' immediate problems so efficiently, prison welfare departments performed an essential service admirably. But, the 'welfare cycle' had at least two unfortunate side effects. One was that prison welfare officers tended to spend most of their time dealing with men who presented concrete problems. Those who were uninvolved with the business of living and who may have sought prison as an escape from the demands of life outside were least likely to have contact with prison welfare departments. This meant that, in effect, they used prison as a shelter and emerged no better equipped to deal with life than when they went in. Of all prisoners, the inadequate's criminality was most likely to be related to social functioning problems and he was potentially in the greatest need of help. Yet, once again, he had fallen through the net. The other ill-effect of the welfare cycle was that it hampered prison welfare officers in fulfilling a rehabilitative role. The prison walls diverted the attention of both inmates and caseworkers from the task of rehabilitation, by creating other problems for them to worry about. While a trained caseworker may do welfare work efficiently, a system which employs highly qualified staff to deal with the simpler problems wastes scarce resources.

After-care and post-release problems

Any good resolutions made in prison are put to the test when a man is released. The purpose of after-care is to tide the ex-prisoner over the difficult transitional period following his re-entry into society, and provide him with support for as long as he needs it. Because many prisoners find the process of reintegration hard, it is probable that they could derive great benefit from after-care. It is therefore important that prisoners perceive it to be a service that is relevant to their needs.

Three-quarters of the sample thought they would have at least one problem when they came out of prison; practical problems associated with the transitional period were usually most in mind. Prisoners gave the impression that they were less worried about post-release problems than they were about their immediate problems in prison. Some seemed to view the future through rose-tinted spectacles; some refused to look to the future at all until it became the present; and others did not intend to change their ways and foresaw little difficulty in settling back into the life they had left.

The use of cards with a range of problems printed on them indicated that other matters, such as avoiding reconviction, keeping away from criminal associates and abstaining from heavy drinking, were also a source of worry to many prisoners, in addition to practical problems: inadequates and heavy drinkers were more worried about the future than the others. This was a disturbing finding, because inadequates were least likely to avail themselves of the welfare department's help in planning for their release.

Most prisoners had heard about after-care, though their conception of the sort of service it provided was rather vague—a vagueness which contrasted sharply with the degree of clarity with which they were able to define the prison welfare officer's role. Approximately one-third of the sample said they intended to contact a probation officer after their release; somewhat less than a third were undecided about whether or not they would make contact, and one-third did not intend to make contact. It has been found that opting for after-care is a reasonably good predictor of post-release action, so probably about one-third of the sample were likely to use after-care when they came out of prison.

Only two factors appeared to influence a prisoner's decision to opt for after-care: one was his previous experience of probation officers and the other was his current contact with a probation officer outside. Prisoners whose attitude towards previous supervision was favourable were more likely to opt for after-care. Similarly, prisoners who were in contact with an outside probation officer were more likely to opt for after-care. Other factors, such as post-release problems, heavy drinking and inadequacy, did not discriminate intending users from non-users, so that those most in need of help were not necessarily the ones who were going to seek it. Prisoners' experience of prison welfare departments did not affect their decision either—indeed, the indications throughout the survey were that prison welfare officers and outside probation officers were not linked together in prisoners' minds, but regarded as members of separate services.

Prisoners who said they intended to contact a probation officer did not have very high expectations of the help they would receive; this, too, contrasted with the expectations they had had of prison welfare officers. Some said they hoped to receive practical assistance, but, for most, existing contact with the probation officer seemed to provide the motivation and prisoners merely hoped that he would provide some kind of background support when it was needed. The outside probation officer was thus regarded differently from his counterpart in prison. The latter was hampered because his attribution of a welfare role inundated him with work; whereas the outside probation officer was assigned a peripheral position in relation to post-release problems, and thereby lacked an opening into the lives of his potential clients.*

---

* This does not imply that outside probation officers are relatively unemployed—quite the contrary. The ex-prisoners who do make contact with the after-care service generate more than enough work for the available resources.

The 'hidden market'

The study provided no evidence that prisoners and caseworkers clashed in their approaches to the problem-solving process. This does not necessarily mean that they had similar approaches, though it may be that these overlapped. But, if a real difference of approach existed, any potential clash was avoided because caseworkers allowed themselves to be drawn into meeting demands for immediate aid. However, the study did provide some evidence that when prison welfare officers and probation officers manage to offer a casework service, they would find a receptive market, capable of extension. One piece of evidence came from the fact, that, when given the opportunity to consider problems other than those created by imprisonment, many prisoners expressed anxiety about matters that the caseworker tended to feel were the real problems. Thus, 44 men were worried about the possibility of reconviction, 30 felt they would have difficulty in settling down, and the difficulties in avoiding criminal associates and keeping off alcohol were mentioned by 27 and 23 men respectively. It may be that prisoners' perceptions of their problems were not so divergent from the caseworkers' as appeared from the first enquiries: many were worried about social functioning problems and this was particularly true of inadequate offenders. It seemed probable that these sorts of worries had been temporarily eclipsed by the more pressing difficulties associated with the transitional period.

Another piece of evidence came from asking prisoners to choose among several printed statements of how the caseworker could assist to prevent their reconviction. Reflective discussion was chosen most often as the best help a prison welfare officer could give: reflective discussion and practical assistance were chosen most often as the best help from outside probation officers. It seemed as if this method of questioning revealed receptivity that had been initially hidden because the prisoners were unaware that probation officers gave insight-oriented help. Though amenable to help which involved more 'talking' than 'doing', prisoners comments showed that they felt 'talking' ought to be supplemented by practical assistance.

Prisoners' views of their offences offered further scope for casework. There was a sense in which they, like the caseworker, linked their crimes to other aspects of their lives. Since the questionnaire only explored a small part of this area it was not possible to make any accurate assessment of the extent to which prisoners shared parts of the casework approach. But it was clear that many prisoners saw their offences as responses to circumstances they found themselves in at the time. Thus, 42 men related their offences to economic, interpersonal or psychological problems. Inadequate offenders were more likely to make this link than other prisoners; and crime, for the former, seemed to be the line of least resistance in the face of overwhelming odds. Some of the men who committed offences with associates felt that their social life had been influential in precipitating them into crime. Of 59 men who had been drinking immediately before they committed offences, a number felt that their crime was linked to a drinking problem. Several of these were elderly, inadequate offenders; some were under 30 and given to periodic bouts of heavy drinking with friends; for some the problem seemed to have got completely out of hand and the offender despairingly described himself as an alcoholic.

Most prisoners appeared to share the general values of society and were only too unhappily aware that they were being edged out in the struggle for survival. However, there was a group of prisoners who made it clear that they had chosen to be different and regarded conforming souls, such as the research worker, as a dull lot. These offenders had not so much abandoned the basic values of, what Wootton has called, an 'acquisitive, competitive, hierarchical, envious society',[2] as abandoned the acceptable modes of being acquisitive. In so far as their criminality represented a moral choice to be different, the scope of casework must be limited.

Unlike most caseworkers, many prisoners felt that chance factors played a large part in crime causation. Most of these seemed to think that chance operated by creating adverse situations which reduced their resistance to temptation. Typically, they felt they had little control over their behaviour once they had been overtaken by events, and a criminal relapse was inevitable. This attitude could create difficulties for the caseworker. For example, offenders might feel that there was little point in looking for 'reasons' further back than the situation which had precipitated them into crime; still less, from their viewpoint, could anything be gained by discussing how such situations might be avoided. Those who felt that they, themselves, had contributed to the creation of these situations were more likely to be receptive to an insight-oriented approach.

Obviously, when it comes to utilising a casework service, a prisoner's approach to problem-solving is only one of many factors which will affect outcome: for example verbal ability and intelligence, are also important.[3] Moreover, it is commonly assumed that prisons can create resistance to treatment, by both inmates and staff. But there was no evidence in the present study of prison welfare officers being boycotted because of prisoners' anti-authority attitudes, and a tentative conclusion was that a sizeable proportion of prisoners might be receptive to casework if prison welfare officers found themselves in a position to offer it. This conclusion is supported by Shaw's finding that most of her experimental group were satisfied with the extended contact they had had with prison welfare officers, and a number had welcomed the opportunity, as one man put it, to 'get down to a problem and thrash it out.'[4] Some were critical, of course, generally complaining that the prison welfare officer had acted like an unnecessarily inquisitive amateur psychiatrist.

The question whether it is worth attempting to extend rehabilitative work in prisons when such institutions create so many practical problems for staff and inmates alike demands consideration. Of all the random allocation experiments done with offenders, those most likely to produce positive results have involved giving some form of treatment to offenders in institutions, rather than in the community. This is somewhat unexpected since treatment is taking place within an artificial environment; the explanation may lie in the fact that prisons isolate their inmates from powerful and adverse environmental forces, and so give them the freedom to examine their lives more objectively. Prison, however, is a decidedly drastic method of reducing the pressure of noxious environmental influences: hostels in the community might serve a similar purpose and have many other advantages.

Some implications of the study for casework in prisons

At a theoretical level, the study had two main implications for casework in prisons. The first was that someone had to deal with the problems imprisonment created, and if prison welfare officers were swamped with these problems they became deflected from the task of rehabilitation. Prisoners needed both immediate practical aid and assistance with the social functioning problems related to their offences. The second implication was that, despite the endeavours of prison welfare officers to tap the 'hidden market' for casework, the prisoners studied seemed generally unaware that caseworkers were available to give insight-oriented help. It is therefore vital that workers manage to establish themselves in a clearly defined casework role if they are to avoid being thwarted by inaccurate expectations of their function. Prison welfare officers and outside probation officers have somewhat different tasks: the former need to free themselves from the welfare cycle, and the latter to demonstrate their relevance to prisoners' post-release and social functioning problems.

At a practical level, there are several ways in which prison welfare officers might be released from the pressure of demands for welfare help. One way woul be to provide other people to undertake the bulk of the practical work: auxiliaries could be employed, or uniformed prison staff might become more involved. Neither idea is new—the Prison Officers' Association has long advocated greater involvement of staff in social work. However, there are problems in division of labour, and caseworkers in other settings have found it difficult to use auxiliary staff efficiently and have tended to resist delegation of work.[5] Whatever the reasons for this, it may be that delegation of practical tasks to an auxiliary deprives the caseworker of openings for talking to clients about personal matters: and moreover, auxiliaries in other settings have expressed dissatisfaction with their role.

Another way of reducing demands for welfare help would be to make imprisonment a less isolating experience. For example, some prisoners could do more for themselves if they were allowed more letters and visits, or if they had access to telephones. Such matters are outside the scope of the present report, and are mentioned only to stress the point that prison welfare departments cannot be developed in isolation from the other prison services.

The study has several implications for ways in which prison welfare officers might establish themselves in a more clearly defined casework role. One important task is to change prisoners' expectations of the job: as long as prison welfare officers are viewed as intermediaries with the outside world they are likely to remain within the confines of the 'welfare cycle'. Prisoners' perceptions of what their problems are need to be enlarged to include those social functioning problems linked with their offences: this, essentially, is what the research worker did when she asked prisoners to consider a range of post-release problems printed on cards. Prisoners also need to be made more aware that prison welfare officers are in a position to offer 'talking' help, and to be acquainted with the relevance of this approach.

It may be that more discussion of prisoners' problems, and presentation of the service available, by prison welfare officers would be useful at the beginning of sentence. Prisoners, unlike many voluntary patients in a psychiatric hospital or applicants to a casework agency, do not expect 'talking' help: they have defined their problems in terms of their current experience and the caseworker may be best able to shift the emphasis by initiating early contact. Perhaps this implies that prison welfare officers in local prisons could usefully develop their skills as a diagnostic team. Some prisoners get very much more of the officers' time than do others whose need for rehabilitative help may be greater. In order to make use of the resources that are available, there is probably much to be gained by the adoption of short-term, focussed casework techniques. The prison setting lends itself to this kind of approach because the time limits are set.

A major implication of this study for casework practice is that a prisoner's contact with the probation officer responsible for after-care is vital if the service is to be used effectively. Work done by prison welfare officers may be wasted if prisoners do not have the support of a probation officer when they test out their good resolutions, and prisoners are less likely to use after-care if, while in prison, they are not in contact with a probation officer. It seems probable that after-care will remain vague and amorphous in many prisoners' minds, unless it is tied down to a probation officer who has made himself known and discussed his role in relation to the prisoner's particular problems. Visiting prisons is not easy for busy probation officers; sometimes it can take the best part of a day to get to the prison and interview one or two men; and, even then, no future contact may be made. However, if more emphasis were placed on this aspect of a probation officer's job it could well pay off.

Prisoners spend a relatively minute proportion of their sentence in contact with prison welfare officers so that any good work done within the seclusion of the welfare office may be neutralised by the opposing forces of the institution as a whole. Prison welfare officers are unlikely to achieve results if their aims run counter to those of the institution. Their welfare role makes an important contribution to the institution's custodial aims, and discipline staff often recognise the prison welfare officers' value in maintaining a 'quiet nick'. A different type of casework, however, might produce results less acceptable to other staff in the institution. If the institution is to afford an environment conducive to successful treatment, all the staff must be involved.

126

The conclusions in this report are tentative: the study was a small, exploratory one, covering a group of 120 prisoners: generalisations on the basis of the data should be made with caution. Nevertheless, many of the findings of the present study are in harmony with Shaw's results[4] and together, the two studies provide some basis for optimism about the development of casework with offenders.

NOTES TO CHAPTER 6

1. Mayer, J. and Timms, N., *The Client Speaks*. Butterworth, 1971.
2. Wootton, B., *Social Science and Social Pathology*. Allen and Unwin, 1959.
3. For example, see Gibby, R., et al *Rorsehach Criteria for Predicting Duration of Therapy*. J Consult. Psych., 18, 1954;
   and, Hilier, E., *An analysis of patient/therapist compatibility*. J. Consult. Psych., 22, 1958.
4. Shaw, M., *Social Work in Prison*. Home Office Research Studies No. 22, HMSO, 1974.
5. A useful discussion of the contribution auxiliary workers can make is contained in a publication by the U.S. Department for Health, Education and Welfare, *Pros and Cons: New Roles for Non-Professional in Corrections*, prepared by Benjamin, J., Freedman, M. R. and Lynton, F., 1966.

APPENDIX I

Basic Information about the Sample

Basic information about the sample was collected from Criminal Record Office.

Age
59 % of the sample were under the age of 30. The sample was compared with the population of male adults imprisoned for indictable offences in England and Wales during 1969. The one sample t-test was applied, which showed that the proportions of under-30s in the sample was representative of the wider population.

Table X1

Age of men in the sample

Age	Number of Men			Total	%	Age	1969 Receptions into Prison in England and Wales*	
	Stafford	Drake Hall	Winson Green				Number of Men	%
Under 24 yrs	27	10	10	47 } 24 ∫	59	Under 30 yrs	14,340	55
25–9	5	11	8					
30–4	3	6	3	12				
35–9	3	3	5	11		30 yrs and over		
40–4	1	3	1	5	41		11,512	45
45–9	1	5	9	15				
50–4	0	1	4	5				
55+	0	10	0	1				
Total	40	40	40	120	100	Total	25,852	100

* Prison Statistics, 1969, Table D.1.: Adult Prisoners under sentence of imprisonment for indictable offences, without the option of a fine.

Stafford inmates were more likely to be under 30 than inmates in Drake Hall ($p < \cdot 01$; 1 df) and Winson Green ($p < \cdot 01$; 1 df).

Number of previous convictions
The table below shows the number of previous convictions men in the sample had.

The sample was compared with the population of men imprisoned for indictable offences in 1969 and the one sample t-test applied. The proportion of men having five or fewer pre-convictions was not significantly different.

Stafford inmates tended to have the least number of previous convictions and Winson Green inmates the most. However, the χ^2 test did not reveal significant differences between the prisons.

Table X2

Number of previous convictions

Number of Previous Convictions	Number of Men			Total	%	Number of Previous Convictions	1969 Receptions	
	Stafford	Drake Hall	Winson Green				Number of Men	%
0	0	1	0	1	} 40	5 or less	8,871	35
1	4	4	0	8				
2	3	2	0	5				
3	4	5	3	12				
4	6	3	3	12				
5	5	2	3	10				
6–9	10	11	12	33	} 59	6 or more	16,589	65
10–14	6	9	7	22				
15+	1	3	12	16				
Not known	1	0	0	1	1			
Total	40	40	40	120	100	Total	25,852	100

Number of previous imprisonments

The men varied greatly in the number of times they had been in prison before. Fifty-one (43%) were experiencing their first sentence of imprisonment, 26% their second or third, while 31% had been in prison from three to over 21 times before. There were also differences between prisons: Stafford inmates were less likely to have had two or more previous imprisonments than inmates in either Drake Hall ($p<\cdot001$; 1 df) or Winson Green ($p<\cdot001$; 1 df). Winson Green inmates were more likely to have had two or more previous imprisonments than those in Drake Hall ($p<\cdot01$; 1 df). Thus the Stafford group had the least prison experience and the Winson Green group the most.

Table X3

Number of previous sentences of imprisonment

Number of Previous Sentences of Imprisonment	Stafford	Drake Hall	Winson Green	Total	%
0	32	15	4	51	43
1	6	7	3	16 }	26
2	2	4	10	16 }	
3	0	6	2	8 }	31
4	0	2	2	4	
5	0	3	2	5	
6–10	0	1	8	9 }	
11–15	0	2	6	8	
16–20	0	0	0	0	
21+	0	0	3	3 }	
Total	40	40	40	120	100

Previous probation or statutory after-care

62% of the sample had been placed on probation at least once. There were no significant differences between prisons.

Table X4

Previous experience of probation

Number of Times on Probation	Stafford	Drake Hall	Winson Green	Total	%
None	16	19	10	45	38
Once	10	10	16	36	30
More than once	13	11	14	38	32
No criminal record	1	0	0	1	
Total	40	40	40	120	100

Fewer men had experience of statutory after-care, i.e. borstal or detention centre after-care; corrective training or preventive detention licence. 36% had experienced supervision under licence of this kind on at least one occasion. There were no significant differences between prisons.

Table X5

Previous experience of statutory after-care

Number of Times Under Statutory After-Care	Stafford	Drake Hall	Winson Green	Total	%
None	21	34	21	76	64
Once	13	6	12	31	26
More than once	5	0	7	12	10
No criminal record	1	0	0	1	
Total	40	40	40	120	100

Current offence

The offences for which men were currently imprisoned were divided into three groups. 68% had committed offences falling into the category of burglary or theft. 16% had been convicted of a motoring offence, e.g. driving whilst disqualified, no tax, no insurance etc.; 16% had been convicted for offences against the person, e.g. indecent assault, wounding, assault. Most of the offences appeared to be rather trivial: few involved large sums of money and most showed a lack of planning and expertise.

Table X6

Current offences

Current Offence	Stafford	Drake Hall	Winson Green	Total	%
Burglary and theft	26	33	23	82	68
Motoring offences (excluding theft of vehicles)	4	7	8	19	16
Offences against the person	10	0	9	19	16
Total	40	40	40	120	100

Most common offence

The predominance of property offenders in the sample is illustrated by the men's most common offence. Offences involving money or property were the most common previous offence of 71 % of the sample. Motoring was the most common offence for 14 % and offences against the person for 8 %.

Table X7

Most common previous offence

Most Common Previous Offence	Stafford	Drake Hall	Winson Green	Total	%
Burglary and theft	27	29	29	85	71
Motoring	4	7	6	17	14
Offences against the person	6	0	4	10	8
Other	2	4	1	7	6
No criminal record	1	0	0	1	1
Total	40	40	40	120	100

APPENDIX II

The Social Functioning Scores

Scales were constructed to assess individual performance in four areas of social functioning: family, work, friends and geographical stability. Scores on these scales essentially measure the stability of, or the individual's commitment to, the activity concerned. Thus a low score on the employment scale denotes lack of commitment to or involvement in work, and a high score denotes a reasonably stable employment record and the individual expressing some interest in the job he was doing.

Information about prisoners' functioning in these four areas was collected by the research worker during the course of the interview. Usually the information emerged, without being specifically requested, when prisoners described their criminal careers. However, when it was not covered in these accounts, the men were questioned on this point. The tables below show the criteria used in coding their answers, and the distribution of the sample on the various scales.

Table X8

Involvement with family/opposite sex

		Number of Men	%
1 point	*Isolate*—no family, girl friend, wife	12	18
2 points	Tenuous relationship with some sort of base: e.g. girl friend whom he may or may not marry; marriage characterised by frequent separations and generally a very unstable affair; e.g. single man who returns to family home spasmodically but has little emotional involvement with its members	34	28
3 points	*Deeper involvement* though some instability: e.g. girl friend or cohabitee of longer standing; marriage showing some signs of strain; family with whom single man lives fairly permanently Main criterion here is, that, despite some degree of instability, the individual would almost certainly bank on the support of his family	30	34
4 points	*Apparently real commitment* to a partner; reasonably stable and satisfying relationship, not, however, without its ups and downs	24	20
	Average score: 2·4 points	120	100

Table X9

Involvement in employment

		Number of Men	%
1 point	*No involvement* Unemployed much or all of the time during the last 12 months. May or may not have 'sidelines' e.g. scrap metal	42	35
2 points	*Superficial involvement* Mostly in work, but continually chops and changes	35	29
3 points	*More involvement* than previous category. Usually in work though not settled in choice of trade	13	11
4 points	*Reasonable degree of involvement* Settled in a particular job or trade and gets some satisfaction out of it. No chopping and changing	30	25
	Average score: 2·2 points	120	100

Table X10

Social involvement

		Number of Men	%
1 point	*Social isolate* No friends or acquaintances to speak of	13	11
2 points	*Semi-isolated* A few acquaintances e.g. pals he knows in a pub	37	31
3 points	*Some social support* Larger number of acquaintances e.g. friends goes drinking with	42	35
4 points	*Reasonably integrated with* some or many people he would call friends	28	25
	Average score: 2·7 points	120	100

Table X11

Geographical stability

		Number of Men	%
1 point	*Vagrant* Does not settle anywhere: no home/no base e.g. moves around the country more or less continually; no fixed abode, within a more limited radius; succession of lodging houses/hostels	12	10
2 points	*Semi-vagrant* e.g. can settle for a while then gets 'itchy feet'; tends to have a base from which he can operate; works for a firm which takes him all round the country	20	17
3 points	*Controlled movement* e.g. army/job; absence of impulsive movement	32	27
4 points	*Settled* Well established in current abode	56	46
	Average score: 3·1 points	120	100

On all except the last scale, the average score was approximately two points—representing marginal involvement in the area concerned.

Scores on the four sub-scales were added together to provide an overall social functioning score, with a possible range of between four and 16 points. For the purposes of analysis the sample was divided into four approximately equal groups, as shown in Table X12.

Table X12

Social functioning scores

Score	Stafford	Drake Hall	Winson Green	Total	%
4–8	5	5	16	27	22
9–10	11	9	10	30	25
11–12	9	11	6	26	22
13–16	15	14	8	37	31
Total	40	40	40	120	100

Two lowest groups against two highest—
Winson Green and Stafford: $p < \cdot 05$; df = 1
Winson Green and Drake Hall: $p < \cdot 05$; df = 1

69% of the sample had total scores of 12 points or less, i.e. scores which represented fairly disorganised living. The average score was 10·5 points, indicating an average score of only 2·5 points on the individual sub-scales. Winson Green inmates were lower scorers than men in either Drake Hall or Stafford.

APPENDIX III

Supplementary Tables

Table X13

Social functioning scores × age

Social Functioning Score	Age		Total
	29 Years and Under	30 Years and Over	
4–10 points	26	31	57
11–16 points	45	18	63
Total	71	49	120

$p < \cdot 01$; df$=1$

Table X14

Social functioning scores × number of previous imprisonments

Social Functioning Score	Number of Previous Imprisonments		Total
	0, 1	≥ 2	
4–10 points	20	34	54
11–16 points	37	29	66
Total	57	63	120

$p < \cdot 001$; df$=1$

Table X15

Social functioning scores × most common offence

Social Functioning Score	Most Common Offence		Total
	Property	Other (Motoring, Violence etc.)	
4–10 points	48	6	54
11–16 points	37	22	59
Total	85	28	113

No one offence the most common: 7

$p < \cdot 01$; df$=1$

Table X16

Mentioned problems in connection with onset or development of criminality × age

Mentioned Problems	Age		Total
	≤29 Years	≥30 Years	
Yes	18	24	42
No	52	25	77
Total	60	59	119

No information: 1

p<·05;   df=1

Table X17

Mentioned problems in connection with onset or development of criminality × most common offence

Mentioned Problems	Most Common Offence		Total
	Property	Other	
Yes	37	4	41
No	48	24	72
Total	85	28	113

No one offence the most common: 7

p<·05;   df=1

Table X18

Mentioned problems in connection with onset or development of criminality × social functioning score

Mentioned Problems	Social Functioning Score		Total
	4–10 points	11–16 points	
Yes	29	13	42
No	27	50	77
Total	56	63	119

No information: 1

p<·001;   df=1

136

Table X19

Marital status × existence of problems during sentence

	Married/Cohabiting	Unattached	Total	%
Mentioned problems	49	39	88	73
Did not mention problems	10	22	32	27
Total	59	61	120	100

p < ·05;   df = 1

Table X20

Use of welfare departments × marital status

A

Marital Status	Number of Contacts						Total
	Stafford		Drake Hall		Winson Green		
	0	≥1	0	≥1	0	≥1	
Married/cohabiting	4	15	2	22	3	13	59
Unattached	8	13	5	11	14	10	61
Total	12	28	7	33	17	23	120

Winson Green: p < ·05;   df = 1

Individual prisons contain similar patterns, though the common pattern is most marked in Winson Green. These patterns are probably better illustrated by showing the percentage of men who had no contact with departments in each of the three prisons:

B

Percentage Having No Contact				Overall Percentage Having No Contact
Marital Status	Stafford	Drake Hall	Winson Green	
	%	%	%	%
1. Percentage of married/co-habiting men having no contact	21	8	18	15
2. Percentage of unattached men having no contact	38	31	58	44
Total	30	17	42	30

In each prison the percentage of married men having had no contact with welfare departments was lower than that obtained for men who were unattached. The difference between the two was greatest in Winson Green.

Table X21
Use of welfare departments × social functioning scores

Social Functioning Score	Number of Contacts						Total
	Stafford		Drake Hall		Winson Green		
	0	≥1	0	≥1	0	≥1	
1. 4–10	5	11	5	11	13	12	57
2. 11–16	7	17	2	22	4	11	63
Total	12	28	7	33	17	23	120

χ^2 for individual prisons not significant.
Overall, men with low social functioning scores were less likely to be users.

$$p < \cdot 05; \qquad df = 1.$$

Table X22
Use of welfare departments × heavy drinking

Presence of Heavy Drinking	Number of Contacts						Total
	Stafford		Drake Hall		Winson Green		
	0	≥1	0	≥1	0	≥1	
Yes	6	10	4	12	12	10	54
No	6	18	3	21	5	13	66
Total	12	28	7	33	17	23	120

χ^2 for individual prisons not significant.
But, overall, heavy drinkers were less likely to be users.

$$p < \cdot 05; \qquad df = 1$$

Table X23

A   Use of welfare departments × inadequacy score

Inadequacy Score	Number of Contacts						Total
	Stafford		Drake Hall		Winson Green		
	0	≥1	0	≥1	0	≥1	
0, 1 Reasonably adequate	4	13	2	14	2	10	45
2 Not very adequate	6	9	0	10	4	4	33
3, 4 Very inadequate	2	6	5	9	11	9	42
Total	12	28	7	33	17	23	120

χ^2 for individual prisons not significant; patterns dissimilar in some ways, though in each the percentage of very inadequate men who were non-users is higher than the percentage of reasonably adequate non-users. Numbers probably too small to make meaningful conclusions.

138

B

Inadequacy Score	Percentage Having No Contact			Overall Percentage Having No Contact
	Stafford	Drake Hall	Winson Green	
	%	%	%	%
0, 1	23	12	17	18
2	40	0	50	30
3, 4	25	36	55	43
Total	30	17	42	30

Table X24

Use of welfare departments × mention of problems to research worker

	Number of Contacts						Total
	Stafford		Drake Hall		Winson Green		
	0	≥1	0	≥1	0	≥1	
1. Mentioned problems	5	21	4	27	9	22	88
2. Did not mention problems	7	7	3	6	8	1	32
Total	12	28	7	33	17	23	120

Winson Green: $p < \cdot 01$; df=1.
χ^2 not significant for Stafford and Drake Hall.

Table X25

Nature of post-release problems anticipated × marital status

	Marital Status		
	Married/Cohabiting	Unattached	Total
1. Mentioned interpersonal problems	17	5	22
2. Did not mention interpersonal problems, but mentioned practical or personal problems	31	36	67
Total	48	41	89

No problems mentioned: 26
Problems other than the above-mentioned: 5

$p < \cdot 05$;   df=1

Table X26

Nature of post-release problems anticipated × social functioning score

	Social Functioning Score		
	4–10	11–16	Total
1. Mentioned interpersonal problems	6	16	22
2. Did not mention interpersonal problems, but mentioned practical or personal problems	38	29	67
Total	44	45	89

No problems mentioned: 26
Problems other than the above-mentioned: 5

$p < \cdot 05$; $df = 1$

APPENDIX IV

The Questionnaire

The questionnaire is given in full. However, the sections on the Post-Sentence Interview and previous experience of supervision were not utilised in the present study.

Interviews stuck fairly closely to the questionnaire. 'Filler' questions, such as what men thought of prison were often asked between the various sections, or at the beginning, as it sometimes proved difficult to sustain a prisoner's interest in social work topics for long at a time. Descriptions of prisoners' criminal careers were usually obtained as the opportunity arose, not necessarily at the end of the interview.

INMATE INTERVIEW

Name ....   Length of Sentence ....

Prison Number ....   Prison ....

C.R.O. Number ....   Date of Birth ....

1. Post Sentence Interview

1. What were you charged with?

2. Can you tell me how it happened? How did you come to do it?
   Associates: YES/NO
   Been drinking/drunk at the time: YES/NO

3. Did you expect to be arrested or did it come as a bit of a surprise? ....
   1. Expected it in the near future—no surprise when it happened.
   2. Expected it would happen sometime—but a surprise when it actually did.
   3. Not anticipated—caught in the act/offence involved the police.
   4. Not anticipated—forgotten/not guilty/thought had got away with it.

4. Were you remanded in custody, or on bail, or were you sentenced straight away?
   1. Sentenced straight away.
   2. Remanded on bail.
   3. Remanded in custody.
   4. Remanded both on bail and in custody.

5. What sort of sentence did you expect to get? ....

6. What did you, in fact, get? ....

7. What did you feel like when you got your sentence? ....
   1. Severely upset/thoroughly sick/felt terrible.
   2. Mildly upset/a bit rough.
   3. Not upset really/not too bad/not really bothered.
   4. Not upset at all/relieved.

8. Was anything worrying you after you'd been sentenced? Did you have any particular problems on your mind? ....

141

9. Had you managed to set your affairs in order or were there things left behind that needed doing? Probe: rent/job/debts etc. ....

10. Did you see a Probation Officer at all after you had been sentenced? YES/NO

11. *If yes:* did you know him? YES/NO..

Content of post-sentence interview

12. Can you tell me what happened when you saw him—what did he say? Did he ask if he could help at all? Did you mention any of your problems to him? ....

13. Probation Officer agreed to undertake action on prisoner's behalf: Yes/No/No action requested ....

14. *If action undertaken*, was prisoner informed of this: Yes/No/No action requested ....
....

15. *If prisoner did not mention problems to Probation Officer:* why didn't you mention problem to him? ....

Opinion of interview

16. Probation Officers have only recently started coming down to the police cells to see people who have been sentenced. Do you think it's a good thing or not, or couldn't you say?
....

17. Did you personally welcome the Probation Officer coming down to see you, or did you resent it, or couldn't you say? ....

18. Did you feel like talking to him, or not, or couldn't you say? ....

19. Did you feel you'd had long enough to talk to him, or did you wish he'd stayed a bit longer?
....

20. How long did he stay with you? ....

2. Prison Welfare Officers

21. Since you've been inside, have you had any problems on your mind, or not? Probe.

Those mentioning problems only

22. Have you discussed this/these things with anyone on the staff in here? Yes..........................
Prison Officer/Chaplain/the Welfare/Governor/Assistant Governor etc. ....
....

23. *If has discussed problem(s):* How did you hope he would be able to help? And what did he actually do?
   a. Problem 1.................................   discussed with ....
   b. Problem 2.................................   discussed with ....
   c. Problem 3.................................   discussed with ....
   d. Problem 4.................................   discussed with ....

24. If had discussed problems with P.W.O.: did you talk about anything else with the Welfare, apart from the problem you went with? ....

25. *If had not discussed some or any problems with P.W.O.:* have you thought of talking to the Welfare about this/these things? *Probe* for reasons why problem not discussed.
   Problem 1. ....
   Problem 2. ....
   Problem 3. ....

142

All

26. Have you had any (other) contact with the Welfare while you've been inside? *Probe:* nature of contact, who initiated it, help wanted (if any), help given etc.
    Contact 1...
    Contact 2...
    Contact 3...
    Contact 4...

27. *If went to P.W.O. with a problem:* did you talk about anything else, apart from the problem you went with? ....

28. How many times have you seen the Welfare altogether whilst you've been inside?
    Prison 1. ....
    Prison 2. ....
    Prison 3. ....

29. On the whole, would you say you were satisfied with the help you received, or not, or couldn't you say?
    Prison 1. ....
    Prison 2. ....
    Prison 3. ....

30. What would you say the Welfare's job is? What sort of things do they do?

31. What's your opinion of the Welfare on the whole? ....

32. What do most people in here think of them? ....

33. Suppose we imagine the Welfare are interested in helping to prevent you from getting into trouble again. What's the best way they could help with this? Or don't you think there's anything they can do to help here?

34. On these cards we have put ways in which the Welfare might help so far as staying out of trouble is concerned. Which do you think is the best way they could help you, or don't you think that any of these would help?
    1. Getting things fixed up for when you go out.
    2. Giving you advice and telling you what to do.
    3. Letting you talk about your worries and get things off your chest.
    4. Helping you think about why you get into trouble and what you might do to avoid it in the future.
    Comments ....

35. Did you know that the Welfare were Probation Officers? YES/NO
    Comments ....

3. Previous Experience of the Probation and After-Care Service

36. Have you ever had any contact with the Probation Service in the past? *Probe:* nature of contact ....

Those with previous experience of supervision under licence only

37. What did you think of probation/borstal after-care etc. with P.O. (name)......................?
    Was it a worthwhile experience? Or rather useless? *Probe:* reasons for answer. Topics of conversation during interviews ....

38. Did you like (P.O.).....................................as a person? Or not particularly? *Probe:* reasons for answer ....

143

39. Did he help with the sort of difficulties you had at the time? (specify)

40. Do you think he helped so far as staying out of trouble was concerned or not? *Probe:* reasons for answer ....

41. Do you think he was typical of most Probation Officers or not? *Probe:* reasons for answer
....

[Questions 37–41 repeated on separate sheets for experience with other Probation Officers]

Those with other contact
42. Did you like the Probation Officer, or not particularly? ....

All
43. What do most people in here think about Probation Officers?.........................

44. Has any Probation Officer been in contact with you whilst you've been inside? *Probe:* nature of contact...

4. After-Care

45. Did you know that Probation Officers were trying to help people when they came out of prison? Have you heard of after-care? YES/NO
    Comments ....

46. Thinking about your own release from prison: what sort of things do you think will be problems for you, or don't you think you'll have any difficulties?..............................

47. These are a collection of things that people sometimes say will be difficult for them when they come out of prison. Can you sort through them and tell me which ones you think will be a problem for you.
    1. Getting work.
    2. Finding somewhere to live.
    3. Not having any clothes or tools.
    4. Paying of debts.
    5. How things will go between you and your wife.
    6. How things will go between you and your family.
    7. Having difficulty in settling down.
    8. Being afraid you won't be able to cope with things.
    9. Feeling that you're on your own.
    10. Getting depressed.
    11. Getting in with the wrong crowd.
    12. Keeping off the beer.
    13. Stopping gambling.
    14. Getting into trouble again.
        Comments...

48. Have you thought of going to see a/your Probation Officer when you come out? ....
    ....

49. *If decided to go:* how do you hope he will be able to help? Or aren't you going for anything in particular?..

50. *If decided to go:* do you think he will be able to help so far as staying out of trouble is concerned? *Probe:* how ....

51. *If decided not to go:* why don't you think you won't make contact?..............................
    ....

144

52. Suppose we imagine that Probation Officers are interested in helping to prevent you from getting into trouble again. What do you think is the best way they could help with this, or didn't you think there's anything they could do to help so far as this is concerned? (exclude if covered in question 50) ....

53. On these cards we have put four ways in which a Probation Officer might try to help so far as staying out of trouble is concerned. Which would you say is the best way they could help you, or don't you think that any of these would help?
    1. Getting things like a job, a place to live, or money or clothes fixed up for when you first come out.
    2. Giving you advice and telling you what to do.
    3. Letting you talk about your worries and get things off your chest.
    4. Helping you think about why you get into trouble and what you might do to avoid it in the future.
    Comments ....

54. Sometimes you hear people say that 'you can never be sure you'll stay out of trouble—it just happens.' Do you agree with this or not? ....

55. Prisoner's account of onset, pattern and development of his criminal career ....
    ....
    (on separate sheet) ....

5. Social Information

56. Marital status at the time of arrest:
    1. Unattached.
    2. Courting.
    3. Cohabiting.
    4. Married and living with wife.
    5. Separated temporarily, living alone.
    6. Separated permanently/divorced—living alone.
    7. Separated/divorced and cohabiting.
    8. Other.
    Comments ....

57. Accommodation at time of arrest:
    1. With parents/siblings.
    2. With wife/cohabitee.
    3. With relatives.
    4. With friends.
    5. Alone/lodgings.
    6. Hostel/no fixed abode.
    7. Other.
    Comments ....

58. Work record over last 2 years of freedom:
    1. Regular (no longer gaps between jobs).
    2. Frequent job change but usually employed.
    3. Frequently unemployed.
    4. Permanently unemployed.
    Comments ....

59. Nature of normal employment ....

60. Friends:
    1. One of a large family, close group of friends.
    2. Large number of acquaintances.
    3. A few acquaintances.
    4. Social isolate.
    Comments ....

Titles already published for the Home Office

11. Thirteen-year-old Approved School Boys in 1962
by Elizabeth Field, W. H. Hammond and J. Tizard. 35p

12. Absconding from Approved Schools
by R. V. G. Clarke and D. N. Martin. 85p

13. An Experiment in Personality Assessment of Young Men Remanded in Custody
by H. Sylvia Anthony. 52½p

14. Girl Offenders Aged 17 to 20 years
by Jean Davies and Nancy Goodman. 52½p

15. The Controlled Trial in Institutional Research
by R. V. G. Clarke and D. B. Cornish. 29p

16. A Survey of Fine Enforcement
by P. Softley. 47p

17. An Index of Social Environment
by Martin Davies. 47p

18. Social Enquiry Reports and the Probation Service
by Martin Davies. 36½p

19. Depression, Psychopathic Personality and Attempted Suicide in a Borstal Sample
by H. Sylvia Anthony. 36½p

20. The Use of Bail and Custody by London Magistrates' Courts Before and After the Criminal Justice Act 1967. 57p
by Frances Simon and Mollie Weatheritt.

21. Social Work in the Environment
by Martin Davies. £1.10

22. Social Work in Prison
by Margaret Shaw. £1.45

23. Delinquency Amongst Opiate Users
by Joy Mott and Marilyn Taylor. 41p

24. IMPACT. Intensive Matched Probation and After-care Treatment: Vol. 1. The design of the probation experiment and an interim evaluation
by M. S. Folkard, A. J. Fowles, B. C. McWilliams, W. McWilliams, D. E. Smith and G. R. Walmsley. 59p

25. The Approved School Experience
by Anne B. Dunlop.

26. Absconding from Open Prisons
by Charlotte Banks, Patricia Mayhew and R. J. Sapsford.

27. Driving while Disqualified
by Sue Kriefman.

HMSO

Government publications can be purchased from the Government Bookshops at the addresses listed on cover page iv (post orders to P.O. Box 569, London SE1 9NH), or through booksellers.

Printed in Scotland by Her Majesty's Stationery Office at HMSO Press, Edinburgh
Dd 506833 K12 7/75 (12299)

16/c086